The legal side of buying a house

a Consumer Publication

Consumers' Association
publishers of **Which?**
14 Buckingham Street
London WC2N 6DS

a Consumer Publication

edited by   Edith Rudinger

published by   Consumers' Association
publishers of **Which?**

Consumer publications
are available from
Consumers' Association
and from booksellers.

© Consumers' Association, March 1983
Amended reprint March 1984

ISBN 0 85202 250 6
and   0 340 33164 X

Photoset by Paston Press, Norwich
Printed in England

contents

STOP PRESS

Following the Chancellor's budget speech on 13 March 1984, in future the stamp duty on buying a house will be 1% of the purchase price above £30,000 (and no longer as given in the text and calculations in this book). (*See particularly pages 21, 72, 83, 98, 106.*)

foreword

Once upon a time – and not all that long ago – it was generally believed that it was illegal or impossible for a layman to do his own conveyancing – that is, buy or sell his house, without employing a solicitor.

Then, in 1965, came the break-through: Consumers' Association published *The legal side of buying a house*, the very first step-by-step guide to conveyancing at its simplest: the typical transfer of a house in England or Wales, wholly occupied by the seller, and with a title that is already registered. It does not deal with new property, or flats (nor with what happens if the house is in Scotland or Northern Ireland where the procedure and the law are quite different).

Since then, so-called do-it-yourself conveyancing has become a fact of life, and Consumers' Association is active in trying to help consumers get a fair deal in all aspects of buying and selling a house.

After a dozen updating revisions of this book, the time has come for this completely new edition, to take account of the changes in the law and procedure, changes in the official forms and documents, and the change in consumer climate, as they affect the parts played by solicitors, building societies, banks, surveyors, local and public authorities (such as the Land Registry) and, of course, the buyer and seller who copes with the legal side of transferring a house unaided, or aided only by this book.

buying a house

Many people ask themselves why should buying a house be more complicated than buying a watch, a freezer, a yacht or a car. The answer lies in the fact that land, which in legal terms includes any buildings on it and everything over and under it, has always been the tangible basis of our social, economic and political life.

Land is permanent, lawyers call it 'real'. It can be handed down from generation to generation, from father to daughter, from uncle to nephew. Two or more people can own the same piece of land at the same time, husband and wife, business partners and any others. Many and various rights can be enforced over it such as rights of way, mineral rights, sporting rights and restrictions as to its use. Land invariably adjoins other land, so mutual rights and obligations arise between neighbours, such as rights of light. These rights and obligations may differ according to how the land is built on, for example houses or flats. And lastly, because the availability of land in our country is limited it is subject to strict governmental controls, planning restrictions, health and safety regulations and many others.

To get an inkling of the complexities of buying a house, imagine buying a new freezer and finding when you got it home, that its boundaries were not clear, that Mrs Brown has a right to put one block of ice-cream in the second freezing compartment every thursday, that you must not use it for storing frozen peas, or that you need planning permission to place a toaster on top of it.

A solicitor has been trained to understand and deal with these complexities and if you employ him, he takes over the responsibility of buying your house. He deals with such matters as thoroughly investigating the seller's title to the house, making appropriate enquiries of government bodies, and ensuring that your transaction is absolutely foolproof so that you may live in your house as you intend.

registered and unregistered land

In England and Wales (the law in Scotland and Northern Ireland is different) all land is either unregistered or registered, and there are two quite distinct methods of transferring the ownership of each. Under the unregistered system, every time the property changes hands, the buyer must make a fresh investigation of the title offered to him. He must satisfy himself as to the validity of the seller's title, that is, his right to sell the property, by investigating the documents of title (known as title deeds) covering at least the past fifteen years, to make sure that the property was correctly transferred to previous owners. This procedure can be extremely lengthy and technical, and it is advisable to employ a solicitor if you are contemplating buying a house with unregistered title.

Towards the end of the last century, an alternative method of conveyancing was introduced into this country, the registered land system; in its modern form it dates from the Land Registration Act 1925. This system is administered by a government department called the Land Registry, in accordance with the terms of the Act and various rules brought out under it. The idea behind the system is that the state guarantees the title, and pays compensation if anything should go wrong in the Registry. Title to property is investigated once only – by the Land Registry. All the details that are material to the title are then recorded on a central register (the Land Register) which is then kept accurate by regular updating of the information in it. This register is the registered owner's proof of title and he receives a copy of the register, called a land certificate, as evidence of his title (or if the property is subject to a mortgage, there is a charge certificate instead of the land certificate).

The result is that by a simple examination of the register, a prospective buyer of registered property should be able to see the exact nature of any rights over, or interests in, the property he intends to buy. This greatly simplifies the buying procedure, although the system does involve a great deal of form filling-in.

Whether or not a property is subject to the registration of title depends on whether it falls within an area of compulsory registration.

The system of land registration has been introduced gradually. Now, approximately seventy-five per cent of the population of this country live in areas where registration of title is compulsory. The compulsory areas include all the large urban parts of the country such as Manchester and West Yorkshire (but huge sparsely populated areas such as Devon and Cornwall still remain unregistered). Even after an area is made an area of compulsory registration, title to property within it does not have to be registered until the next time it is sold. Only thirty per cent of actual land in England and Wales is registered.

It has always been government policy to extend the registered system to the whole of England and Wales. For a time, progress slowed down considerably, but the government now hopes to have compulsory land registration in the whole of England and Wales by 1994.

is it registered?

If you want to find out whether registration is compulsory in any particular place you can ask the Land Registry (Lincoln's Inn Fields, London WC2A 3PH, telephone 01-405 3488) for explanatory leaflet no. 9, which they will send you free of charge. This leaflet sets out the districts in England and Wales in which registration is compulsory and gives the district Land Registry for each county. A supplement to leaflet no. 9 (also free, but you have to request it specially) shows the date on which a particular area became a compulsory registration area. The longer a particular area has had compulsory registration of title, the more likely it is that a particular property there is registered. Eastbourne was made a compulsory area in 1926 and most property there is now registered, having been sold at least once since 1926. However Arun, not many miles away, was only designated a compulsory area in 1978, so comparatively few properties there will have registered title as yet.

Until 1966, a person could voluntarily register his title in a non-compulsory area, but with very limited exceptions this is no longer possible for a private individual.

You can tell whether your title is registered if you have a large folder entitled 'Land Certificate' with your deeds. If you have bought your property with the aid of mortgage, the folder will be entitled 'Charge Certificate' (but it will be held by your building society or other mortgagee).

when to use this book

The object of this book is to describe in detail the procedure to be followed
where an owner-occupier is selling a house with registered title to a person
who wants the house for his own occupation. To this end we will follow an
imaginary buyer, Matthew Seaton, who will guide us step by step through
the buying of a house, 14 Twintree Avenue, Minford.

when you should use a solicitor

This book does not deal with the buying and selling of unregistered
property. Nor does it cover a newly-built house, especially where it is part
of a housing estate.

IF NEWLY-BUILT HOUSE

For a newly-built house, the buyer's solicitor must ensure that the contract
provides that the house itself should be properly built. He must make sure
that the boundaries are correctly shown on the plans, that the seller is
providing any right of way, drainage rights and similar rights which may be
necessary and that the restrictions imposed by the seller are fair. Once
these matters are settled for the first buyer, they are fixed more or less
unalterably for the future, so that a subsequent buyer's solicitor is in the
position of having to take things as they stand. He has to explain them to
his client, but the legal work involved in a second or subsequent purchase
is much less than on the vital first purchase.

IF PARTS ARE LET

Complications can arise, primarily under the Rent Act legislation, where
part of the property is let and the buyer is taking over a sitting tenant. In
this case, it is advisable to consult a solicitor.

IF BUYING A COUNCIL HOUSE

A new procedure has been introduced under the terms of the Housing Act
1980 for local authority tenants to buy their council house. Such a purchase
is not dealt with in this book; buyers can obtain help in this from the housing
department of the relevant local authority.

FOR SOME LEASES

The procedure described in the book is inappropriate, too, for cases where
a person takes a lease at a rent (not a ground rent) without paying a capital

sum. This does not mean that leasehold property is excluded from consideration here. It is quite common, especially in London, to find a house where an owner-occupier is the holder of a lease which he has bought for a capital sum, that is, the property is leasehold, not freehold. Legal difficulties do arise at the time when the lease is first granted, usually when the house is first built, and such cases are outside the scope of this book. However, once the lease is granted and assuming that the title to it is registered (which it must be where the lease is granted for a term of at least 21 years and it falls within a compulsory registration area) the procedure is much the same as the sale of a freehold. The terms of the lease may be a little more difficult to understand and the process of buying more lengthy, because some extra investigations could be necessary.

FLATS AND MAISONETTES
The buying of a flat or maisonette is also outside the ambit of this book. Although the title to a flat may be registered, many problems can arise with the enforcement of mutual rights and obligations and use and maintenance of common parts of the building, and also the exterior of the building.

BUSINESS PREMISES
Finally, business premises are excluded; totally different considerations apply to them.

you can do it yourself
Provided that the house (which includes terrace or semi-detached houses, cottages and bungalows) is a secondhand one, at present fully occupied by an owner-occupier and the title to it is registered, there is no reason why an ordinary person should not be able to buy and sell it without employing a solicitor. If you decide to buy your own house, you can save yourself a substantial amount of money in solicitors' fees. Although solicitors no longer charge a scale fee for conveyancing, they generally charge a fee in the region of two per cent of the purchase price. So, on the purchase of a house of £50,000 you could save upwards of £1000 in fees. Furthermore, if you are buying the house with the aid of a mortgage, you can also save the solicitor's fee for dealing with the mortgage. But, as we shall discover from Matthew Seaton's purchase of 14 Twintree Avenue, all other expenses will have to be paid, including stamp duty, Land Registry fees and the building society's solicitor's fee.

When selling by yourself, you will again save a solicitor's fee. Few, if any other expenses are involved in selling, except that where you have a mortgage to pay off, you generally have to pay a fee to the building society's solicitor (of around £20–£30).

BUT BEWARE
Having decided to do your own conveyancing either on buying or selling a house, it is important to realise that it may prove impossible for you to succeed in carrying it through. In guiding the imaginary Matthew Seaton through his purchase and sale we have to point out many of the pitfalls, legal or otherwise, that may occur. If one or other of these problems makes it impossible for you to continue with your own conveyancing, you should immediately consult a solicitor. He may charge you the same fee he would have charged had he handled the transaction right from the beginning and may be scathing of your efforts so far. But you should not let this deter you from going to him, if you are in any real doubt or difficulty.

Outline conveyancing procedure for buying a house

		SENT BY	SENT TO
1.	Application for mortgage	buyer	building society (or other lender)
2.	Instruction to surveyor	buyer	his surveyor
3.	Draft contract with an 'office copy' of the entries on the register and filed plan	seller	buyer
4.	Enquiries before contract (form Conveyancing 29 Long LM Revised)	buyer	seller
5.	Local Search (forms LLC1 and Con29A England & Wales, Con 29D London)	buyer	local authority
6.	Answers to enquiries before contract	seller	buyer
7.	Mortgage offer	building soc	buyer
8.	Surveyor's report	surveyor	buyer
9.	Local search certificate and replies to enquiries	local auth	buyer
10.	Negotiation and approval of draft contract	buyer / seller	seller / buyer
11.	Exchange of contracts	buyer	seller
12.		seller	buyer
12.	Authority to inspect the register (form 201)	seller	buyer
13.	Requisitions on title (form Con 28B)	buyer	seller
14.	Draft transfer (form 19 or 19(JP))	buyer	seller
15.	Answers to requisitions on title	seller	buyer
16.	Approval of transfer	seller	buyer
17.	'Office copy' of entries, filed plan, contract, enquiries before contract, requisitions on title, local authority search, authority to inspect the register, draft transfer	buyer	building society
18.	Requisitions on title	building soc	buyer
19.	Answers to requisitions on title	buyer	building society
20.	Draft mortgage deed	building soc	buyer
21.	Completion statement	seller	buyer
22.	Mortgage deed	building soc	buyer
23.	Land Registry search (form 94A)	buyer	Land Registry
24.	Land Charges search (form K16)	buyer	Land Charges
25.	Land Registry search certificate	Land Registry	buyer
26.	Land Charges search certificate	Land Charges	buyer
27.	Completion		
28.	Transfer to be stamped within one month (form Stamps L(A) 451)	buyer or building society	Stamp office or head post office
29.	Transfer to be registered (form A4)	buyer or building society	Land Registry

CONVEYANCING

Buyer

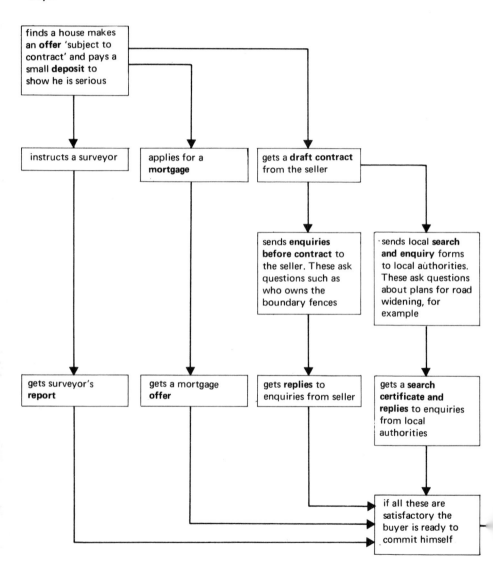

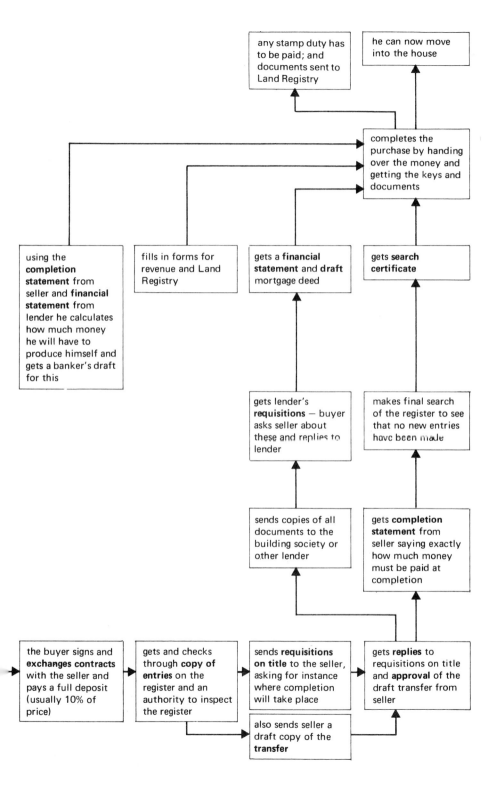

any stamp duty has to be paid; and documents sent to Land Registry

he can now move into the house

completes the purchase by handing over the money and getting the keys and documents

using the **completion statement** from seller and **financial statement** from lender he calculates how much money he will have to produce himself and gets a banker's draft for this

fills in forms for revenue and Land Registry

gets a **financial statement** and **draft** mortgage deed

gets **search certificate**

gets lender's **requisitions** — buyer asks seller about these and replies to lender

makes final search of the register to see that no new entries have been made

sends copies of all documents to the building society or other lender

gets **completion statement** from seller saying exactly how much money must be paid at completion

the buyer signs and **exchanges contracts** with the seller and pays a full deposit (usually 10% of price)

gets and checks through **copy of entries** on the register and an authority to inspect the register

sends **requisitions on title** to the seller, asking for instance where completion will take place

gets **replies** to requisitions on title and **approval** of the draft transfer from seller

also sends seller a draft copy of the **transfer**

10

The main participants

THE BUYER
Matthew J. Seaton,
38 Broadstone Drive,
Hastings, Sussex.

THE SELLER
William H. Timms,
14 Twintree Avenue,
Minford, Surrey.

THE SELLER'S SOLICITORS
Dodds & Son,
1 Charter Street,
Minford, Surrey.

THE BUYER'S BUILDING SOCIETY
Forthright Building Society,
88 Lomax Street,
Minford, Surrey.

THE SELLER'S BUILDING SOCIETY
Minford Building Society,
102 Great Winchester Street,
Minford, Surrey.

THE BUYER'S BUILDING
 SOCIETY'S SOLICITORS
Hodgson, Green & Co.,
67 Lomax Street,
Minford, Surrey.

THE SELLER'S BUILDING
 SOCIETY'S SOLICITORS
Anderson, James & Pringle,
88 Great Winchester Street,
Minford, Surrey.

THE BUYER'S INSURANCE
 COMPANY
Bridstow Insurance Co Ltd,
403 High Street,
Guildford, Surrey.

THE SELLER'S ESTATE AGENTS
Flint & Morgan,
43 High Street,
Minford, Surrey.

THE BUYER'S SURVEYORS
Andrew Robertson & Co,
22 Hamilton Street,
Minford, Surrey.

finding a house

Matthew Seaton, a young schoolteacher, and his wife Emma, a newly qualified veterinary surgeon, have been saving hard to buy a house of their own since they got married five years ago. Just after Christmas, Matthew learnt to his great surprise that a distant relative of his had died and left him a legacy of £5000. This added to their savings meant that they now had about £9000. Matthew had spoken with the manager of the Forthright Building Society (with whom they were saving) and learnt that taking into account both his and Emma's current earnings, he should have no difficulty in obtaining a mortgage for £32,000, provided that the property they decided to buy was considered satisfactory. Now they would start seriously looking for a house.

A few days ago they had received particulars of 14 Twintree Avenue, Minford, Surrey, from Flint & Morgan, one of the firms of estate agents they had been dealing with. They had gone to see the house immediately and had fallen in love with it. Mr Timms the seller wanted £40,000 for the house and although he refused to accept anything lower, he did agree to include all the curtains and fitted carpets at present in the house in this price. He had hoped to sell these separately. £40,000 was the limit Matthew and Emma had set themselves, but they liked the house so much and were happy with the arrangement over the curtains and carpets, so they decided to buy it.

the estate agent

The next day Matthew went into Flint & Morgan's offices and told Mr Morgan that he wished to buy 14 Twintree Avenue. Mr Morgan was expecting him, he had already spoken on the telephone with his client. He also knew all about the curtains and carpets. He asked Matthew if he would leave a small deposit. This is quite normal procedure and shows that you are a serious buyer, but check that you are dealing with a reputable firm of estate agents before you actually hand any money over.

Matthew agreed to leave a cheque for £100 and Mr Morgan said that he would sent him a receipt for this by post. If you pay such a deposit in cash, you should obtain a receipt on the spot. It is as well to make clear that payment of such deposit is 'subject to contract and survey' just in case something goes wrong later.

It is useful to ask the estate agent at this stage whether the title to the house is registered, whether anyone other than the seller and his family are living in the house (for example a tenant), and the name of the local authority. Mr Morgan did not know whether the title was registered but assumed that it was, since Surrey had been a compulsory registration area since 1952 and he thought that Mr Timms had only lived in the house for about ten years. He told Matthew that the local authority was Minford District Council and confirmed that no-one other than Mr Timms was living in the house.

Mr Morgan then enquired which firm of solicitors would be acting for him in his purchase, to which Matthew replied that he was doing his own conveyancing. Mr Morgan would pass this information on to Mr Timms' solicitors, who are responsible for getting the conveyancing ball rolling.

mortgage application

To-day, the 'cash buyer' is a very rare animal. Most of us need additional finance to buy a house and Matthew was no exception. You do not need a solicitor's help to apply for a mortgage although he may be able to advise you on where to go for a loan if the particular circumstances of your case make it difficult for you to obtain finance in the ordinary way. For example, a building society may refuse you a mortgage because of your advanced years or because the property you want to buy was built before 1914. The estate agent who is selling the house can also be helpful in finding a number of sources. He probably has an extra incentive to help: he may get a commission from the body providing the finance when a mortgage is successfully negotiated. (Some agents have arrangements with financing bodies that if they introduce a prospective borrower, they will be paid a small commission if the loan is made.) And he will get his selling commission from the seller on the sale of the house which a mortgage has made possible.

Matthew had decided to get his loan from the Forthright Building Society where he and Emma had their savings invested. Other possible sources of finance for buying a house are banks, insurance companies, some local authorities and private lenders. The Consumer Publication *Raising the money to buy your home* deals with the whole subject in detail and takes the reader through the steps of applying for a loan.

From whatever source a loan is sought, it will take some time to make the arrangements. Forms must be filled in and most lenders check references to verify a buyer's financial position and prospects. They will also want to have the property inspected, to make sure that it is one on which they would be willing to advance a loan.

Matthew therefore went straight from the estate agents to see the manager of the Forthright Building Society and told him that he hoped to buy 14 Twintree Avenue and would like to apply for a loan from the society of £32,000, approximately 80 per cent of the purchase price. The manager gave him an application form. This asked for information regarding himself and the house. He was also given another form requiring him to list any persons who would be living in the house and inform the society of any change before the loan was made.

valuation and survey
The manager then explained to Matthew that once he had received the application form completed by Matthew, he would instruct the society's surveyor to make arrangements to inspect the house and prepare a valuation report. All building societies and most other lenders require such a report before lending money on the mortgage of a house. The property is the security for their money; if a buyer defaults on repayments, they must make sure that the proceeds of sale of the property would be sufficient to reimburse them.

The buyer has to pay the surveyor's fee which, though no longer on a fixed scale, is generally based on the purchase price of the house (not the amount of the loan). Matthew learnt that he would have to pay a valuation fee of £58.65 (including VAT). It is important to realise that a survey made on behalf of a building society or other lender is for the purpose of valuation and is not necessarily adequate for a buyer, who would be well advised to obtain an independent structural survey.

In the past, a buyer was never allowed to see the valuation report although he pays for it. Building societies do not guarantee that a house is structurally perfect (or even fit for human habitation), although you would probably have some come-back if the house actually collapses.

Nowadays, offers of advance may expressly exclude any warranty as to the state of the property. The reasoning is that the surveyor is acting for the building society or other lender when he prepares a valuation report, not the buyer of the house and because of this some building societies do not even tell buyers the value the surveyor has placed on the property.

If the building society's valuation report is made available to you, treat it with caution. Remember that all the society or lender is interested in is the value of the property; major defects may be overlooked. Under our law a buyer is subject to the rule of *caveat emptor* (buyer beware!), even when it comes to buying a house. A buyer takes property subject to any defects which he could have discovered by inspection by an expert eye whether or not an expert inspection has taken place. That is why it is advisable to have an independent survey carried out, by a reputable surveyor.

Matthew asked the manager of the Forthright Building Society to let him know which firm of surveyors would be preparing the valuation report, so that he could instruct them to do an independent survey of the house for his own benefit.

It is quite normal to employ the same surveyors as are preparing the valuation for the building society. You will probably save some money on fees by doing this, as there need be only one visit by one professional surveyor to the house. If the surveyor is on the staff of the building society he may not be able to carry out a private structural survey at the same time. On the other hand, some building societies have introduced a choice of basic, 'middling' and full survey, in conjunction with their valuation-survey (and the borrower pays accordingly).

The cost of the independent survey should be agreed in advance. It depends on the size of the house and the time spent there and how thorough a survey is required. If the house is still furnished at the time when the surveyor is to make his examination, he will not be able to make as detailed a survey as if the house were empty. The surveyor may advise against buying the house unless he is given the chance to make a thorough examination.

It is not only with old property that it is desirable to have a survey done. A recently-built house can have serious defects too, through bad design, bad workmanship or neglect or a combination of these.

For a small fee, or even without an extra fee, a surveyor will sometimes advise the buyer on the value of the house. But a scale fee is payable by the buyer if he himself asks for a formal valuation.

the correspondence starts

The next day Matthew received the first letter to go on his file. It is advisable to keep a file of all correspondence, documents and so on regarding your purchase. They will also come in useful on any re-sale.

FLINT & MORGAN
Surveyors
Estate Agents

43 High Street
Minford, Surrey

4th January 1983

To: M. J. Seaton Esq

Dear Sir,

Re: 14 Twintree Avenue, Minford

We confirm your call at this office today, when you agreed to proceed with the purchase of the above property from our client W. H. Timms Esq, at the price of £40,000 to include curtains and carpets, subject to contract and survey. We confirm that you have paid a preliminary deposit of £100 for which we enclose our receipt. We understand that you intend to deal with the legal formalities yourself. Messrs Dodds & Son of this town will be acting as solicitors for Mr Timms and will contact you in due course.

We confirm that the title to the property is registered.

Yours faithfully,
Flint & Morgan

A formal receipt was enclosed.

the forms you will need
It is as well to obtain all the forms you will need for your purchase well in advance from Oyez Publishing Ltd, who publish legal books and documents. There are Oyez shops in Birmingham, Bristol, Cardiff, Manchester, Sheffield, Leeds, Liverpool and London, where the forms can be bought. Or they can be ordered by post.

These are the forms you will need:

2 prints of Enquiries before contract (Conveyancing 29 Long LM Revised)
2 prints of Requisitions on title (Con 28B)
2 prints of Enquiries of district councils (Con 29A England and Wales; for London, the form is Con 29D London)
2 prints of Register of local land charges Requisition for search and official certificate of search (LLCI)
3 prints of Transfer of Whole (19) (For property being bought by joint buyers ask for form 19(JP) instead of form 19)
1 print of Application by purchaser for Official Search with priority in respect of the Whole of the land in a title (94A)
2 prints of Application to register dealings with the Whole of the land comprised in registered titles (A4)
1 print of Application for office copies (A44)
1 print of Application for an official search of the index map (96)
1 print of Application for an official search (Bankruptcy only) (K16)

Matthew telephoned Oyez House (01-407 8055) to find out the cost of these forms. He then wrote to Oyez Stationery Ltd, Oyez House, 237 Long Lane, London SE1 4PU listing the forms he required and requesting them to be sent to him as soon as possible. He enclosed a cheque for £6 which included postage, packing, VAT and handling charge for what Oyez calls the 'conveyancing pack'.

All but the first three of these forms can be bought from Her Majesty's Stationery Office. The only other form needed is a land valuation form L(A) 451 which can be obtained from some post offices (you can find out which ones in your area by enquiring at your local head post office) or Inland Revenue Stamp Office, Bush House, Strand, London WC2B 4QN.

the mortgage application
Matthew now completed the application form for a mortgage from the Forthright Building Society. On the supplementary form headed 'List of Intended Occupants' he inserted the name of his wife Emma, and signed the part requesting him to inform the society of any change prior to an advance. He then posted the forms, together with a cheque for the valuation fee of £58.65, to the manager of the society.

If a house is to be bought in joint names of husband and wife, or any other two people, this should be made clear in the mortgage application and both must sign the form.

A few days later he received an acknowledgement to his mortgage application.

FORTHRIGHT BUILDING SOCIETY

88 Lomax St
Minford, Surrey

7th January 1983

To: M. J. Seaton Esq

Dear Sir,

Re: 14 Twintree Avenue, Minford

We thank you for returning the application for an advance, and for the cheque for £58.65 in respect of the valuation fee. The Society's surveyor is arranging to inspect and report as soon as possible.

The firm of surveyors who will prepare the valuation are Messrs Andrew Robertson & Co, 22 Hamilton Street, Minford. I have spoken to Mr James Robertson on the telephone and he will be glad to carry out a survey of the house for you at the time of doing our valuation. He is expecting instructions from you on this matter.

I enclose a receipt for the valuation fee.

Yours faithfully,

M. C. Templeton,
Manager

THE INDEPENDENT SURVEY

On receipt of the letter from the manager of the Forthright Building Society, Matthew phoned Mr James Robertson to arrange a structural survey to be carried out on his behalf, and agreed a fee of £150.

He wrote confirming his instructions:

38 Broadstone Drive,
Hastings, Sussex

To: Messrs Andrew Robertson & Co   10th January 1983

Dear Sirs,

<u>14 Twintree Avenue, Minford</u>

I confirm my instructions given on the telephone that you should carry out a survey on the above property on my behalf.

We agreed that your fee should be £150 on the basis that you are also preparing a valuation for the Forthright Building Society in connection with my purchase of this property. We further agreed that, as well as making the usual examination you will examine and test the drains and the electrical wiring in the house. If it proves necessary to obtain the assistance of a plumber or electrician, their charges will be in addition.

I further confirm that I hope to have your report within a fortnight.

Yours faithfully,

M. J. Seaton

draft contract

On wednesday, Matthew heard from Dodds & Son, Mr Timms' solicitors

DODDS & SON	*1 Charter Street*
Solicitors	*Minford, Surrey*

To: M. J. Seaton Esq   11th January 1983

Dear Sir,

Re: 14 Twintree Avenue, Minford

We understand that you propose to purchase the above property from our client Mr W. H. Timms at the price of £40,000 (to include curtains and carpets) subject to contract and survey, and that you have paid a preliminary deposit of £100 to our client's agents, Messrs Flint & Morgan. We further understand that you propose to act without a solicitor on your purchase and have informed our client of this.

   We enclose a draft contract together with a copy for your use. Enclosed also are office copies of the entries on the register and filed plan.

Yours faithfully,
Dodds & Son

   Under the council of the Law Society's rules of conduct, a solicitor should point out to his client (in this case, the seller) that he is dealing with an unrepresented person and that this could lead to complications and delay, even where this is quite unlikely to be the case. But it may persuade a seller to seek a sale elsewhere.

   Dodds & Son had enclosed a draft contract. Most solicitors in England and Wales use a printed form of contract, either the National Conditions of Sale or the General Conditions published by the Law Society. These printed forms, when completed, contain the usual terms of a contract, such as the parties (buyer and seller), the property, the price, the deposit and so on. They also lay down many lengthy and detailed conditions which cover the rights of the parties in almost every conceivable circumstance.

   The seller's solicitor decides which of the two sets of conditions should govern a particular transaction. Both sets of conditions enjoy equal popularity. Until quite recently, only solicitors could buy them, but now they can be bought by members of the public from law stationers.

   The draft contract Matthew received incorporated the National Conditions of Sale. It was on a pale blue piece of paper, folded down the middle to form four pages and, on the inside, twenty-two standard conditions were laid out. He was pleased that Dodds & Son had sent him a spare copy. It is normal practice to send two copies of any document in draft. The recipient keeps one copy for his own file and sends the other back with suggested amendments, if any.

the National Conditions
The first page of the contract was headed 'CONTRACT FOR SALE. The National Conditions of Sale, Twentieth Edition' and consisted of a series of panels in which the basic details of the transaction had been filled in. The top panel contained the full name and address of the 'Vendor', Mr Timms and the 'Purchaser', Matthew. He checked to see that these were correct.

The second panel was divided into two: on the left-hand side was a box headed 'Registered Land' and in here Dodds & Son had typed the District Land Registry, Tunbridge Wells and the title number: SY 43271604.

Directly underneath this was a box for the 'Agreed rate of interest', and this was typed in to be '11 per cent per annum or 2 per cent above the base rate of Barclays Bank plc from time to time whichever shall be the higher.'

PRESCRIBED RATE OF INTEREST
If no rate of interest is specified, under the standard conditions printed on the inside of the form, condition 7 says that it shall be the 'prescribed rate'. This is laid down intermittently by the Treasury by statutory instrument: the *Acquisition of Land (Rate of Interest after Entry) Regulations*. The current rate is published in the *Solicitors' Journal* and the *Property Law Bulletin* (available from most law stationers) whenever the rate is changed. You can telephone the offices of the *Solicitors' Journal* to find out about the latest change.

The 'agreed rate of interest' is important to both buyer and seller. It governs how much interest a buyer has to pay on the balance of the purchase price if he completes the purchase later than the agreed date or is allowed to go into possession of the property before completion.

DEPOSIT
In the right-hand box, £40,000 had been typed in against 'Purchase price'; underneath this was the heading 'Deposit'. Condition 2 of the standard conditions provides that a buyer shall pay a deposit of ten per cent of the purchase price to the seller's solicitor on the date the contract is made. The 10 per cent includes any 'earnest money' paid to the estate agents as soon

as a price is agreed. You may be allowed to pay less than a 10 per cent deposit, in which case there will be a special condition typed in on the back of the form, stating the amount. However, the seller may be unwilling to accept less than 10 per cent, because if he does and the contract comes to an end through no fault of his own, he cannot sue for the full 10 per cent deposit as damages.

Condition 2 further provides for the deposit to be held by the seller's solicitor as stakeholder. This means that he may not give the deposit (or any part of it) to the seller without the buyer's permission. A special condition (on the back of the form) may require that the deposit should be paid to the solicitor as 'agent for the vendor', which means that he does not have to retain it until completion and would have to pass it on to the seller if asked to do so. If you find such a special condition on your draft contract, ask the other side if it can be removed, so that the deposit is held by a stakeholder.

Matthew had already paid £100 to Flint & Morgan, the estate agents, so he would have to pay a further £3,900 when the contract became binding on him at exchange of contracts. This was likely to be in two or three weeks time.

'CHATTELS', AND STAMP DUTY

Against 'Price fixed for chattels' would be written the figure, if one had been agreed, which the buyer was paying for items such as any furniture or perhaps a freezer or a lawnmower which the seller was leaving behind and the buyer buying. It does not include fixtures and fittings which are part of the house, such as central heating radiators.

Often it is useful, and indeed quite normal practice, to agree and state separately the value of items the seller is leaving behind, in order to reduce the purchase price and consequently the stamp duty payable when the house is eventually transferred. The Consumer Publication *Which? way to buy, sell and move house* includes a discussion of what constitutes fixtures and fittings.

Stamp duty is payable to the government on certain documents, including deeds transferring houses. No stamp duty is payable on the transfer of a house where the price is not more than £25,000. Where the price is between £25,000 and £30,000 the stamp duty on the transfer is one half per cent of the purchase price. Where the price is between £30,001 and £35,000 the duty is one per cent; between £35,001 and £40,000 the duty is one and one half per cent; over £40,000 the duty is two per cent.

Thus, in Matthew's case if the purchase price had been £41,000 it would have been perfectly reasonable for him to agree to buy the curtains and carpets separately from Mr Timms at the price of £1000. This would have been typed against 'Price fixed for chattels', and if Dodds & Son had forgotten to do this, he could have asked them to amend the draft contract accordingly. He would then save himself £220 in stamp duty because stamp duty is payable on the price of the house only, and not on extras such as furniture, and also because the additional £1000 would have brought the purchase price over the next percentage threshold. Stamp duty can be saved in this way only where the price is genuinely arranged before the contract becomes binding, and only where it can be honestly said that the price for the chattels bears a reasonable approximation to their true value.

WHAT THE VENDOR SELLS

Next came a large panel in the contract form in which, under the heading 'Property and interest therein sold' there had been filled in a description of the property itself: 'Freehold dwelling house and premises situate at and known as number 14 Twintree Avenue, Minford, Surrey.' It is solicitors' wont to use such a formula of words; but there is no need to say more than '14 Twintree Avenue, Minford, Surrey; freehold'.

If the house had been a leasehold one, there would have been included here a reference to the lease: its date, who granted it originally and to whom, the period covered by the lease and the ground rent. The part of the heading 'interest therein sold' refers to whether the property is freehold or leasehold and if leasehold, the particulars of the lease. In Matthew's case, the house was said to be freehold and as this was what he had previously understood, this was acceptable.

Directly underneath the description of the property was a thin panel with the words 'Vendor sells as'. Here the seller must state the capacity in which he is selling the property. Mr Timms was selling as 'Beneficial Owner'. This means that the property belonged to him and that the legal title to it was vested in him. Where property is co-owned by husband and wife they usually sell as beneficial owners, too. Occasionally property is sold by 'trustees for sale', which means that two or more people are holding the legal title to the property on trust to sell it and distribute the proceeds. If you are buying from trustees for sale, it is important to make sure that at least two of them are parties to the deed actually transferring the property, otherwise, when it comes to selling the house again, you may have difficulty in proving your title to the next buyer.

Very rarely you may come across someone selling as 'tenant for life'. Here the seller is entitled to enjoyment of the property (called settled land) for his lifetime only. After his death, it passes to others in accordance with the terms of an existing will or trust (called a settlement). Buying from a tenant for life is more complicated than buying from a beneficial owner. You must check that the person you are dealing with is the registered owner and that at least two trustees of the settlement are made a party to the eventual transfer (making three parties on the selling side). Where land is settled or held on trust for sale, you will find a restriction on the documents of title to the effect that any proceeds of sale from the property must be given to at least two trustees, and naming them.

THE DATE FOR COMPLETION
Further along the same panel was a space for inserting the proposed completion date. The actual date was left blank at this stage, and would be arranged when matters were a little more advanced. Matthew hoped to move in as soon as possible and had in mind that the date for completion should be about four weeks after exchange of contracts.

The standard conditions provide (in condition 5) that if no date is inserted in the contract, completion should take place 26 working days after exchange of contracts or delivery of the seller's proof of title, whichever is the later. Under the conditions, a 'working day' is any day from monday to friday inclusive, with these exceptions: Christmas day, Good Friday, a bank holiday and a day on which the Treasury orders the suspension of financial dealings.

DO NOT SIGN YET
The bottom panel of the contract form contained a brief summary of the whole document: 'Agreed that the vendor sells and the purchaser buys as above, subject to the special conditions endorsed hereon and to the National Conditions of Sale Twentieth Edition so far as the latter conditions are not inconsistent with the special conditions.'

Immediately underneath was the space for signing the contract when the time came, and dating it.

Matthew knew that he should not be tempted to write in ink on the spare copy of the contract which Dodds & Son had sent him. The spare copy would eventually be the actual contract which he would exchange with Mr Timms.

the special conditions

Matthew now turned the contract form over. The back was headed 'Re: 14 Twintree Avenue, Minford, Surrey: Timms to Seaton' and was devoted to the 'Special conditions of sale'. Clause A referred to condition 3 of the standard conditions on the inside page, which only applies if clause A says it does. Condition 3 gives the buyer a limited right to terminate the contract and recover his deposit if, after the contract is made binding, a matter comes to light which substantially reduces the value of the property, provided that it was not in existence at the date of the contract and was not something which the buyer could have found out for himself. In the event of this occurring, a buyer has to inform the seller or his solicitor in writing of his intention to terminate, within 16 working days of the date of the contract, otherwise he loses the right. (An example of this might be a bus route being changed, after the contract is made, with a major bus-stop being put right outside the house.)

This condition is extremely wide and is not likely to be included in the contract by most sellers' solicitors. Dodds & Son had specified that 'Condition 3 of the National Conditions of Sale shall not have effect'. Matthew made a mental note to be especially thorough when making enquiries about the property and to ask Mr Timms if he could look round it again. He felt he had been sensible that he had arranged for an independent survey to be carried out.

Clause B began 'Title shall be deduced and shall commence as follows:' Next to this had been typed 'The vendor's title shall be deduced in accordance with section 110 of the Land Registration Act 1925'. This requires the seller to supply the buyer with the documents necessary to prove his title, once contracts have been exchanged.

These documents include an authority to inspect the register, 'office copies' of the entries on the register and any filed plans (an office copy is an authenticated copy of an official document issued by the department or organisation which holds the original), copies of any documents noted on the register which are relevant to the property, and copies of documents creating, or evidence of any rights affecting, the property which are not required to be registered, for instance where the seller has granted a lease of the property of less than 21 years.

Matthew patted the office copies of the entries on the register and filed plan which Dodds & Son had sent him and decided to study them in detail after he had finished reading the contract form.

Clause C then went on to say that 'the sale is with vacant possession'. This meant that the house would be completely empty when Matthew completed the purchase and no tenants or lodgers or any refuse such as discarded furniture would be there when Matthew came to move in. If the house had been subject to an existing tenancy, full details of it would have been given here, and in such a case you should seek the help of a solicitor. Matthew thought that if there was any undue delay, he might want or need to take possession before completion, provided Mr Timms agreed. He did not have to suggest that anything be added to clause C to cover this: condition 8 of the standard conditions specifically sets out the rights of the buyer and of the seller should this happen.

Clause D of the special conditions of sale dealt with planning law, under which you are not allowed to make changes in the use of property without planning permission. Clause D said that the property was sold on the understanding that its currently permitted use was use as a dwelling house. Matthew would only be allowed to use it as a house to live in. If, for example, he wanted to use it as an office, or convert it into two flats, or turn the ground floor into a veterinary surgery for Emma, he would have to apply for, and get, planning permission from the local authority. If it should happen that the use specified in special condition D is not the authorised use, at any time before completion (for example, if the use stipulated in the special condition was 'residential and office use' and it is discovered later that the permitted use of the premises is residential only), under condition 15 of the standard conditions, the buyer can terminate the contract and recover his deposit.

Special condition E on the contract form had been crossed out. Here would have been listed the items (had there been any) which Mr Timms was selling separately to Matthew and the agreed price, which would have been additional to the price of the house.

Finally, clause F read as follows: 'The property is sold subject so far as they are subsisting and capable of being enforced or of taking effect to the restrictions and stipulations contained in a transfer dated the 14th day of June 1960 and made between Minford Estate Developments Limited ('the company') of the one part and Bernard Simon Isaacs of the other part. A copy of the said covenants conditions and stipulations having been supplied to the purchaser he shall be deemed to purchase with full knowledge thereof and shall raise no requisition or enquiry with regard thereto.' Matthew looked at the office copies Dodds & Son had sent him and saw that a copy of the restrictive covenants was indeed included. He would study these shortly.

Having got to the end of the draft contract, he realised that Dodds & Son had forgotten to mention the curtains and carpets. He made a note to add a special condition to the draft stating that the curtains and carpets at present on the property were to be left behind and were included in the purchase price.

the Law Society's contract for sale

If your seller's solicitor has sent you a draft contract form incorporating the Law Society's General Conditions of Sale, the first difference you will notice is the colour of the form: it is on a green piece of paper instead of pale blue. The paper is folded down the middle to form four pages and the general conditions are laid out on the inside two pages in the same way as the National's standard conditions. The general conditions cover much the same areas as the National ones do, but they are numbered differently and in some instances their content differs, especially where time limits are concerned. The more important of these differences are mentioned here and will be again as Matthew's purchase proceeds.

The front page is headed 'The Law Society's Contract for Sale (1980 Edition)' and is divided into panels but with a different layout from that of the National conditions. The first panel begins 'Agreement made the . . .' with a space for inserting the date when the contract is made. After the word 'Between' the seller's name and address will be typed against 'Vendor' and the buyer's against 'Purchaser'.

Then follows a brief summary of the transaction; 'It is agreed that the vendor shall sell and the purchaser shall purchase in accordance with the following special conditions the property described in the particulars below at the price of   '. The price at which you have agreed to buy the property will be typed in here.

The second panel contains a description of the property under the heading PARTICULARS in the same terms as the description of 14 Twintree Avenue under the National contract form. This is followed by a printed instruction to see the reverse side of the form for the special conditions of sale.

Then comes a thin panel, on the left-hand side of which will be typed the purchase price, deposit, and price (if any) that you have agreed to pay to the seller in addition to the purchase price for any items he is leaving behind. General condition 9 provides that a deposit of 10 per cent of the purchase price should be paid to the seller or his solicitor as stakeholder on exchange of contracts. However, unlike condition 2 of the Nationals, it adds that such deposit should be paid by a solicitor's cheque or banker's draft. Obviously you will have to use the second alternative. A banker's draft is a cheque signed by a bank manager (or one of his staff) so there can be no doubt that it will be met on presentation. You should inform your bank in advance that you will be needing a draft for the deposit, so that exchange of contracts will not be delayed unnecessarily. You can go to any branch of your bank (take identification with you); your own bank will be notified, and you can collect the banker's draft from any branch you specify.

To the right of this is a box for signing the contract when the time arrives. In the last panel on the first page will be typed the name and address of the vendor's solicitors and local authorities. As you are buying your house without the help of a solicitor, the space for the name of the 'Purchaser's solicitors' will be left blank.

The special conditions relevant to your particular transaction will be on the back page of the contract form, which is headed SPECIAL CONDITIONS. These are different to the ones on the National contract form. Clause A states that 'the property is sold subject to the Law Society's 1980 general conditions of sale printed within so far as they are not varied by or inconsistent with these special conditions' and that 'general condition 8(4) shall apply in any event'. Condition 8(4) applies to the transfer of a leasehold house only. When the property is eventually transferred, the seller impliedly promises (in the deed of transfer) that all the terms of the lease have been complied with to date. The buyer and seller may agree to modify this promise at contract stage, but condition 8(4) stipulates that if they do this, it must be noted on the register.

Next, clause B says that for the purposes of the following general conditions '1(a) the contract rate is   %'. Here you will find the equivalent to 'The agreed rate of interest' on the front page of the National contract form. This will probably be 11 per cent per annum or 2 per cent above the base rate of Barclays Bank plc (or, of course, Midland Bank, or any other stipulated bank) from time to time whichever shall be higher. A figure must be inserted here, because the 'contract rate' under the general conditions, which would apply in the absence of a special condition, is now probably invalid as it is linked to the Bank of England minimum lending rate which has been abolished.

'1(b) contractual completion date is ………. 198   '. This will be left blank to be filled in nearer the time. If no date is agreed for completion, the general conditions provide that completion shall take place on the first working day after five weeks have elapsed from the date of the contract. Under the Law Society's general conditions, working day means any day from monday to friday (inclusive) even if the Treasury has suspended financial dealings on that day. Excluded are Christmas day, Good Friday and any other statutory bank holiday or day which the special conditions state not to be a working day.

'21(5)(a) the latest time is   am/pm' will usually be filled in to say that you must complete the purchase by at least 2.30pm on the agreed completion date. This is to ensure that the seller's solicitor can pay the purchase monies into the seller's bank that same day, which is especially important in a chain transaction. If no time is specified, general condition 21(5)(a) says that the latest time is 2.30pm. If you are late, you are deemed not to have completed until the next working day, in which case you may be charged interest on the balance of the purchase price.

'1(e) the following are not working days' allows space to list specific days (if any) which the seller wants to make non-working days.

'5(3) the following is retained land': condition 5 refers to rights which the seller wishes to retain out of the land sold, for the benefit of some other land of his. Normally, where a seller owns a large piece of land and sells off part, certain rights (called quasi-easements: for example, a right of way) which exist over that part at the time of sale, will pass to the buyer on the transfer to him of that part, without special mention in the deed (and the seller will lose the right). In the contract, the seller must state any land retained by him for the benefit of which he is keeping (in lawyer's language 'reserving') any such rights.

In the space allowed, there should be a description of any adjoining or nearby land retained by the seller (perhaps by reference to a plan which shows all the plots that will enjoy the benefits of the rights reserved).

Next, clause C will probably state that condition 4 shall not apply. Condition 4 is similar to National condition 3 and gives the buyer the right to terminate the contract where certain matters affecting the property come to light after the contract is made. It gives the buyer a right to rescind within 4 weeks of the contract if a matter comes to light that was in existence before the contract was made but which was not within the buyer's knowledge. It includes financial charges, such as road repairs, restrictions on the use of the property, and anything else likely to reduce the value of the property materially – which could cover virtually anything, for example a right of way. Condition 4 puts the seller under a disadvantage because he cannot be sure until four weeks have elapsed from the contract that the buyer will not rescind. Most sellers' solicitors will want to exclude condition 4 because it is very wide. This means that you must inspect the property carefully and make thorough enquiries about it.

Clause D which says 'The vendor shall convey as   ' will probably be completed: 'beneficial owner', but it may be 'personal representative', 'trustees for sale' or 'tenant for life', as explained earlier.

Clause E will tell you the title number under which the property is registered and the district land registry. It will also state the class of title; this is dealt with a little later in the book. The alternative clause E will be crossed out because it applies to unregistered land.

Clause F will state either that the property is sold with vacant possession, or list details of any existing leases or tenancies. If you find the alternative (F) filled in, showing that the property will not be sold with vacant possession, do not proceed with the deal without consulting a solicitor.

Finally, clause G will inform you of any restrictions, and so on, the property is sold subject to, in much the same way as Matthew was told in clause F of his draft contract.

contract races

A solicitor is sometimes instructed by a seller to deal with more than one potential buyer at a time, sending a draft contract to each, which sometimes results in a race to exchange contracts. The practice is not viewed kindly by the legal profession and the Law Society have now made it obligatory for the seller's solicitor to inform the buyer or his solicitor whenever more than one draft contract has been sent out. Certain steps that Matthew takes after he receives his draft contract can be speeded up; for example enquiries can be made personally at the local authority or before you receive the draft contract. It is further possible to exchange contracts before obtaining your independent survey and even before your offer of mortgage advance. The contract would then have to be made conditional on your obtaining a 'satisfactory survey' or 'satisfactory mortgage'. However, if you are seriously contemplating this, you should consult a solicitor.

the 'office copy' of the entries on the register

Matthew now took up the office copies of the entries on the register and the filed plan which Dodds & Son had sent him with the draft contract. An office copy is an official photocopy of the entries made by the Land Registry on the register; it states the district Land Registry it was issued from, and the date on which it was made. The purpose of sending office copies to the buyer or his solicitor is to prove the seller's title: that the property belongs to the seller and that he is able to transfer it to the buyer. Technically, the seller's solicitor does not have to produce such evidence of title until contracts are exchanged. However, since he does have to send to the buyer, with the draft contract, an office copy of any restrictions and other rights affecting the property, and these will normally be noted on part of the register, he invariably sends an office copy of the whole of the title at this stage. It can also save him time and trouble later, and help to avoid any delay on completion.

The register is the registered owner's proof of title. The register of every property is divided into three parts: the property register, the proprietorship register and the charges register.

the property register

The property register contains a description of the property and the 'estate' for which it is held, that is, either freehold or leasehold. It normally refers to a filed plan or to the Land Registry's general map, based on ordnance survey, to complete the identification of the property. Except when boundaries are noted as fixed, the filed plan indicates the general boundaries of the property only and cannot be used to determine disputes as to precise boundaries.

If the property is leasehold, brief particulars of the lease are given including its date, who granted it, to whom, the date from when the lease runs, and for how many years, and any ground rent payable. The register does not set out the lease in full, even though it is a very important document. However, if you are buying a leasehold house you will be provided with a copy of the lease with the draft contract, and you should read this through carefully.

The property register also includes a description of any rights which go with the house, such as a right of way over another property. Such a right forms part of the property itself and it may constitute a valuable asset which enables the occupier to live in, or use the house more effectively. That is the reason for its registration in the property register.

the proprietorship register
This contains the name and address of the person registered as being the registered owner: the registered proprietor. Under the heading 'Proprietorship Register' should appear the words 'Title Absolute'. This implies that the person whose name is entered in the register is guaranteed to be the owner and his title to the property cannot be challenged. This is the advantage of having a registered title. The first person to register has to show that he really is the owner, to the satisfaction of the Land Registry. When he does so, he is registered with title absolute; the best title.

LESSER TITLE
It is possible for an applicant to fail to satisfy the requirements of the Land Registry about title. If this happens, the registry may allow the applicant to register his title but not with title absolute; he will instead be given what is called a possessory title. If a person is registered with 'possessory title' or 'qualified title' it means that no guarantee is given by the Land Registry as to the title. Thus the position of a buyer is similar to a buyer of unregistered land (and he should not do his own conveyancing, but should instruct a solicitor). In the case of leasehold property, the heading to the proprietorship register may state that the owner is registered with title absolute or with good leasehold title. In practice, good leasehold, unlike possessory title, is acceptable.

NO PRICE?
Irrespective of whether the title is leasehold or freehold, the proprietorship register may contain a statement of the price paid for the property by the owner. Because of this, the seller may cut the price out of the copy of the proprietorship register he sends to the buyer and not hand the snippet over until after exchange of contracts – until the buyer has legally committed himself to a price. Otherwise the buyer might be influenced in deciding what price he should pay. For property that has been sold since 1976, the Land Registry has followed this practice and omitted the price, so in some cases, entries may not now include the price.

When a property changes hands the Land Registry adds the new owner's name to the proprietorship register and just strikes through the name of the seller. There is no need for the seller to prove title again nor the buyer to worry about it: when the Land Registry adds the new owner's name to the proprietorship register, the Registry transfers the guarantee of title to the next owner. The proprietorship register often consists of a list of names and addresses and prices paid, all but the last of which have been struck through. The name that is left, is the name of the current registered proprietor.

CAUTIONS
The proprietorship register would also contain the details of any cautions, restrictions or inhibitions which affect the registered owner's powers of dealing with the property. Entry of a caution, restriction or inhibition is the method of protecting an interest in registered land which is not itself registrable. For example, a tenant for life is entitled to settled land for his life only, and it then passes to others (called 'remaindermen'). The tenant for life will be the registered proprietor, but to protect the interests of the remaindermen, a restriction will be entered in the proprietorship register to the effect that the property can only be dealt with in a manner authorised by the Settled Land Act. This includes sale, so the property can be sold, but any proceeds of sale must be paid to at least two named trustees of the settlement (to ensure that the tenant for life does not abscond with the money).

We shall come across an example of a caution a little later in the book. Protection by inhibition, which is very rare, suspends dealings with the property until further notice by the Land Registrar. An example would be where a proprietor's land certificate (evidence of title) has been stolen.

the charges register
This part of the register contains details of rights which other people have over or in respect of the property, which are themselves registrable interests. They are rights and interests which detract from or take something away from the owners property as described in the property register, and are often referred to as incumbrances. The two kinds most commonly found are restrictive covenants and mortgages.

RESTRICTIVE COVENANTS
Restrictive covenants have long been a feature of conveyancing. Where a land owner sells off a large piece of land which is to be turned into a housing estate, he usually requires the developer to undertake that certain condi-

tions shall in future be complied with; for example, he may insist that not more than so many houses to the acre should be built on the land. Likewise, the developer, when he comes to sell off the new houses to the first owners, may require each of them to undertake that the houses should not be turned into a shop, or that no new building be built on the land without the consent of the developer. In both cases, these restrictions are made in the form of written covenants set out in the deed that transfers the property from the seller to the buyer. The buyer is said to enter into restrictive covenants with the seller and the object is usually to do this in such a way that not only the first buyer but all subsequent owners also should be bound by the covenants. Normally the covenants are quite reasonable and unlikely to prevent a buyer from doing anything he wants to do with the property. They can be of advantage to the individual house owners, because they generally operate throughout the neighbourhood.

There is some uncertainty in legal circles about just how far restrictive covenants can be enforced once the property has changed hands. However, a house buyer should assume that all the covenants set out in the charges register can be enforced against him when he becomes the owner.

If you find the restrictive covenants which affect your proposed new house unpalatable, you should consult a solicitor (or look for another property).

The charges register deals with restrictive covenants by setting out a list of the deeds which contain them, and the covenants themselves are set out in full in a schedule at the end of the register.

Particulars of any mortgages are also shown on the charges register, by an entry in two parts for each mortgage. The first states the date of the charge and of registration, and the second states the name of the owner of the charge – generally the building society or other lender.

the office copy of the entries on the register for 14 Twintree Avenue

This is what Matthew saw when he looked at the office copy of the entries on the register which Dodds & Son had sent him.

HM Land Registry
Edition 1   Title Number SY43271604
Opened 4.7.60   This register consists of three pages

A. Property Register
containing the description of the registered land and the estate comprised in the title

---

ADMINISTRATIVE AREA   PARISH OR PLACE
(county, county borough etc)
Surrey   MINFORD
The freehold land shown and edged with red on the plan of the above title filed at the Registry, registered on 4th July 1960 being land and building on the east side of Twintree Avenue. Property now known as 14 Twintree Avenue.

(space for further entries)

B. Proprietorship Register
stating the nature of the title name address and description of the proprietor of the land and any entries affecting the right of disposal thereof.
Title Absolute

Entry no	Proprietor etc	Remarks
~~1.~~	~~Bernard Simon Isaacs, Bus Driver, of 8 Ruddigore Road, Minford, Surrey~~	~~Price paid £400 Registered 4 July 1960~~
2.	William Herbert Timms, Electrical Engineer, of 15 Chapel Lane, Minford, Surrey	Price paid £8,700 Registered 17th November 1971

C. Charges Register
containing charges, incumbrances etc adversely affecting the land and
registered dealings therewith.

The date at the beginning of each entry is the date on which the entry was
made on this edition of the register.

Entry number   Remarks

1. 4th July 1960 – A transfer of the land in this title dated 14th June 1960
by Minford Estates Developments Limited (Vendor) to Bernard Simon
Isaacs (Purchaser) contains restrictive covenants. A copy of the covenants
is set out in the schedule of restrictive covenants annexed hereto.

The schedule before referred to

1. No further buildings shall be erected on the said land.

2. No alterations or additions to the present building shall be made
except in accordance with plans and specifications to be approved by the
vendor or his architect at the expense of the purchasers or their successors
in title.

3. Not at any time to carry on or suffer to be carried on the said land or
any part thereof any trade or business whatsoever or permit the same to be
used for any purpose other than as a private dwelling house and private
garage in connection therewith and not to allow any portion of the property
to be used for the purpose of advertising and not to do or permit or suffer
to be done anything upon the land which may be or become a nuisance or
annoyance to the adjoining houses or to the neighbourhood.

4. The garden ground of the dwelling house shall at all times be kept and
maintained in a neat and proper order and condition as flower or ornamen-
tal gardens and shall not be converted to any other use whatsoever.

2. 17th November 1971 – Charge dated 1st November 1971 registered on
17th November 1971 to secure the monies therein mentioned.

3. Proprietor: Minford Building Society of 102 Great Winchester Street,
Minford, Surrey registered on 17th November 1971.

(blank space for further entries)

Any entries struck through in red are no longer subsisting

Issued by the Tunbridge Wells District Land Registry showing the subsisting entries on the Register on 5th January 1983.

He checked the description of the property in the property register and looked at the filed plan to make sure that it corresponded to the property he wanted to buy. He then verified, from the proprietorship register, that Mr Timms was the registered proprietor with title absolute, and saw that there were no entries limiting his powers of selling the property. If you find that the name on the register is not that of the seller, you should seek the help of a solicitor.

The charges register involved a little more reading. None of the restrictive covenants listed in the schedule seemed troublesome to Matthew. However, he made a note to check that there had been no alteration or addition to the house since July 1960 without the approval of Minford Estates Developments Ltd. If this had happened, their consent would have to be obtained when the property was transferred to Matthew, and it was Mr Timms' job to make the arrangements necessary to obtain such consent and bear the expense involved in so doing. Actually, Matthew did not remember seeing anything built on the property which did not look as if it was part of the original house but he would ask Dodds & Son, just in case.

The other entry in the charges register related to Mr Timms' existing mortgage. This would have to be paid off when Matthew's purchase was completed, and he would have to make sure that the Minford Building Society would not have any right to claim that the house was still mortgaged to them once it had become his property.

Finally, he noted that the office copies had been 'Issued by Tunbridge Wells District Land Registry showing the subsisting entries on the Register on 5th January 1983.'

Matthew heaved a sigh of relief. It had taken him a good part of the morning to read through the draft contract and office copies. He put the office copies away in his file safely; he would need these when making his 'requisitions on title' after exchange of contracts.

Before he could approve the draft contract, he would have to have the answers to certain enquiries he would make of the seller and the local authority.

enquiries before contract

A sale of land often produces a conflict of interests. A buyer naturally wants to find out all he can about the property, good or bad, whereas a seller, albeit willing to sing its praises, may not be so keen to disclose its faults.

THE SELLER NEED NOT SAY ANYTHING

On a sale of land the general rule (known as the *caveat emptor* – buyer beware – rule) is that a buyer enters into the contract at his own risk. However, some good faith is required on the part of the seller in that he must disclose some, if not all, of the facts material to the property. He is under a duty to disclose any latent defects in title. These are incumbrances and other adverse matters of title which the buyer could not discover by himself on reasonable inspection; for example the restrictive covenants on 14 Twintree Avenue we have just looked at. (This is why Dodds & Son mentioned them in the draft contract and sent a copy to Matthew.) But the seller is under no duty to disclose patent defects in title. These are third-party rights of which there is some visible indication on the property and so can be discovered on inspection; such as a path running across land signposted 'public right of way'.

Lastly, a seller need not disclose any physical defect, latent or patent (a latent physical defect might be a damaged flue; a patent physical defect, a missing chimney). But if he does say something about the quality of the property and this turns out to be untrue after exchange of contracts, it may amount to a misrepresentation entitling the buyer to end the contract and/or claim damages.

Because the seller's duty of disclosure is very limited, the buyer or his solicitor presents the seller's solicitor with a list of questions about the property, before contracts are exchanged. These are known as enquiries before contract, or preliminary enquiries. They are usually made on a printed standard form, with any particular enquiries added and (occasionally) inappropriate enquiries struck out.

THE ENQUIRIES

To make his enquiries, Matthew used the same printed form as most solicitors do: *Enquiries before contract (Conveyancing 29 Long) LM (Revised).*

Fourteen of the questions under the heading GENERAL ENQUIRIES apply to all properties and deal with such subjects as ownership of boundaries, disputes (with neighbours, for instance), main services (gas, water and electricity), rights of way and similar rights, occupation by persons other than the seller, restrictive covenants, planning, outgoings on the property, and when completion can be expected.

The fifteenth question on the form headed 'New Properties' applies only to newly-built houses and covers some of the particular problems that arise in such cases.

Then follows a blank space for any additional questions. In the case of a straightforward sale of an owner-occupied house which has registered title, extra enquiries are rarely made. In less simple cases, especially with unregistered land, points may occur to the buyer's solicitor on which he needs extra information or assurance.

The back of the form lists five extra printed questions which apply to leasehold property only. These deal with whether the lease is a head lease (one where the lessor owns the freehold) or an underlease (one where the lessor himself owns the property under a lease, out of which the present lease is carved, granted by a superior lessor who usually owns the freehold); the names and addresses of the lessor, any superior lessor, their respective solicitors, and the agents (if any) to whom ground rent is paid; whether a lessor's consent is necessary for a sale and if so what steps have been taken to obtain this; whether the seller has broken any covenants in the lease (a lease contains many and various obligations, called covenants which have to be observed by both lessor and lessee); whether the requirements of the lease about painting and doing other work have been honoured; details of insurance which under the terms of a lease may have to be placed with a particular insurance company; and whether or not there are office copies of the lessor's title with the deeds. (This will either be the freehold title or any superior lease.)

Question 3 regarding service charges is likely to be inapplicable to a leasehold house.

Again, there follows a space for additional enquiries.

MATTHEW'S ENQUIRIES

At the top of the form, Matthew wrote 14 Twintree Avenue, Minford, Surrey. Underneath was a space for writing the names of the seller and buyer. Matthew needed replies to all but the last two of the fifteen general enquiries on the form (question 14 is only relevant where the seller lives outside the United Kingdom and is selling property he owns here). He therefore crossed out questions 14 and 15 and in the space for additional enquiries he asked 'Since 14 June 1960, has any alteration or addition been made to the house which required consent under covenant No. 1 in the schedule to the transfer of that date? If so, please confirm that any necessary consent has been obtained and will be handed over on completion.'

Restrictive covenants are catered for in question 9 of the general enquiries but Matthew wanted to draw Dodds & Son's attention to this specific covenant in favour of Minford Estates Developments Ltd. He did not want to be in a position where he himself would have to apply for approval of something which Mr Timms, or perhaps his predecessor, had done to the property. Worse still, he did not want to have to restore the property to its original condition.

Had Matthew not received a copy of the filed plan with the draft contract, he would have requested one here.

He then signed and dated the form of enquiries before contract and sent them, in duplicate, to Dodds & Son with a covering letter.

38 Broadstone Drive
Hastings, Sussex

To: Messrs Dodds & Son

13th January 1983

Dear Sirs,

Re: 14 Twintree Avenue, Minford

Thank you for your letter of 11th January enclosing a draft contract relating to my proposed purchase of the above property, and 'office copies' of the entries on the register and filed plan. I am grateful for the copy of the draft contract for my use.

I enclose some preliminary enquiries with a copy.

Yours faithfully,

M. J. Seaton

local searches

That same day, Matthew prepared and sent off an application for a local search, and also enquiries to the local authority.

A local search is an application for an official certificate showing the entries on the local land charges register at the date of the search. The local land charges register is set up to record all public matters that affect property. These matters are restrictive of an owner's use of his land, in the sense that the restriction promotes public welfare (for example, a tree preservation order), as against benefitting an individual. Local land charges are registered by the local authority or other relevant public body, such as a local water authority. A local search reveals such things as listed buildings, long and short term planning schemes and financial charges. For example, where a local authority carries out compulsory repairs to a house under the Housing or Public Health Acts, it will register a charge to recover the cost. A buyer will want to ensure that this has been paid before he completes his purchase. A search certificate speaks only as to the state of affairs on the day of its date. It is important to realise that after that date a change may occur that alters the whole picture.

Other warnings may be contained in the register. A new improvement line may have been made in the area: the local authority maps out an area and draws a line down a particular street to widen the road, say, to ease the flow of traffic. If you are contemplating buying a house in this street, you may loose part of your garden and have to rebuild the garden wall.

Or if there is an opencast coal mine or quarry nearby, a land charge may be registered zoning the area as one prone to noise and disturbance, in which case the relevant authority has powers to compulsorily acquire any land it wants in the area.

Needless to say, a prospective purchaser is therefore usually anxious to receive his local search.

WHERE TO SEARCH
A local search is made with the local district council or in London the appropriate borough council. In Matthew's case, it was Minford District Council. He used form LLC1 (*Register of local land charges Requisition for search and official certificate of search*). He wrote the name of the council in the space at the top of the form: Minford D.C.

Form LLC1 has a printed duplicate of itself attached, to be torn off and retained by the local council, the original only being sent back with the signed certificate on it. Both parts must be filled in.

The register of local land charges is divided into 12 parts and a buyer may apply for a search in just those parts with which he is concerned. But the almost universal practice is to apply for a search of the whole register, which is what Matthew did. To achieve this he crossed out the words 'Parts . . . of' on the form to make it read: 'An official search is required in the register of local land charges'.

In filling in the form it is seldom necessary to do more than describe the property by its postal address; in Matthew's case 14 Twintree Avenue, Minford, Surrey was sufficient. Where the property can only be identified by a plan, a copy of the plan should be sent with the form.

Matthew signed the form and wrote his name, address and telephone number in the panel provided. The cost of obtaining a local search certificate is £2.65.

MORE ENQUIRIES

With form LLCI he sent an application for answers to a number of additional enquiries of the local authority on a form called '*Enquiries of District Councils*'.

Whereas a local search reveals particular public matters affecting a property, these latter enquiries offer a buyer a more general view of what is going on in the area, as they give details of such matters as roads, main services, drains and sewers, planning and conservation.

There are two different editions of this form for use with the different sorts of local authority. If the house is in the area of a district council, the enquiries should be made on form Con 29A England and Wales (white). For a house in the Greater London area, the search must be with the appropriate London borough council on form Con 29D London (buff). Check that the form you use is an up-to-date one (marked '1982 edition').

The form runs into 8 pages, concertina type. It is divided into two parts: part I and part II enquiries. All the questions in part I are answered automatically by the local authority, but part II enquiries are only answered if the enquirer indicates, by placing his initials alongside the question, that he wants to have an answer. The cost of obtaining replies to part I enquiries is £9.65 and for each part II enquiry 75p.

The significance of most of the enquiries on the form (and the replies to them) is quite easy to appreciate. Many of them are self-explanatory, relating to matters such as building regulations, or drains and sewers. Some are not relevant where the property is to be used as a dwelling house; or (as question 13) not applicable unless the buyer is moving into, for instance, a Tudor mansion. The others are likely to affect a buyer such as Matthew.

Of the part I enquiries, question 1 relates to roads and footpaths and will inform you whether or not you are likely to incur any expense in their maintenance. The box for the description of the property, on the front of the form, has a space in which the user is invited to enter details of roads etc to which question 1 is to relate, in addition to the road given in the address.

You should therefore wait until you have a plan of the property, before sending off your enquiries; the plan will show you whether there is a return road frontage or even a rear access passageway of which you should check the maintenance responsibilities. Question 2 also relates to roads but will reveal the proximity of major roads and constructions, for example fly-overs, which could interfere with your enjoyment of the property.

Next, question 3 will tell you about the condition of the property; for example whether it is subject to a repair notice for faulty guttering. Question 5 is about the drainage of the property and the reply will tell you whether you must pay the cost of connecting the property up to, or maintaining, sewer facilities.

Questions 6 and 11 relate to planning. The reply to question 6 will disclose whether the property is free from enforcement proceedings regarding planning. Where something is done in breach of planning control (this can be either building work or changing the use of property) the local authority can take proceedings to have the breach rectified, which in the case of a building may mean taking it down. Every local authority keeps a register (open to public inspection) of enforcement proceedings relating to land in its area, commenced after 27th November 1981. That means any enforcement or stop notice served or issued after 27th November 1981 will be noted. There is a right to appeal against enforcement proceedings.

The answer to question 11 will tell you what planning applications have been made in the area, and the results. Again, a register is kept of these applications and it is open to public inspection. If the property is in the area of a district council, the register is kept by the district planning authority; if in Greater London, by the common council of the City of London or the relevant London borough council.

Finally, question 14 is important because it relates to compulsory acquisition. No buyer should buy a property which is likely to be compulsorarily acquired by a public authority.

Two part II enquiries which are useful to make are 6 and 8. Enquiry 6 concerns unfinished developments. By serving a completion notice, the local planning authority can terminate planning permission for a development if it is not completed within a certain period. This means that the development must be removed if not completed in time.

Enquiry 8 will reveal the proximity of pipe-lines to the property (gas, water, electricity, etc). Where there is a pipe-line, you are not allowed to put up any building or structure (for example a greenhouse) within ten feet of the surface of the land over the pipe-line, without permission.

Matthew filled in Con 29A asking for replies to the part I enquiries and enquiry 8 (which he initialled) of the part II ones (enquiry 6 was not relevant, because Twintree Avenue was not an unfinished development).

He then sent both forms to Minford District Council at the council offices. He enclosed a cheque, payable to the council, for £12.90.

A local authority can take as little as about two weeks to return the local search certificate and replies to enquiries (but some, particularly London boroughs, sometimes take considerably longer).

replies to enquiries before contract

Dodds & Son sent back Matthew's enquiries before contract with their replies quite quickly.

DODDS & SON
Solicitors

To: H. J. Seaton Esq

Dear Sir,

1 Charter Street
Minford, Surrey

17th January 1983

Re: 14 Twintree Avenue

We enclose our answers to your preliminary enquiries and look forward to hearing from you with the draft contract duly approved as soon as possible.

Yours faithfully,
Dodds & Son

Unfortunately, it is the tendency of some vendors' solicitors to give non-committal and meaningless replies to preliminary enquiries. They fear making inaccurate representations about the property which may result in the sale being frustrated (because misrepresentation may entitle a buyer to rescind the contract and not go ahead with the purchase). This risk has been greatly increased by the Misrepresentation Act 1967. However, the current trend amongst good solicitors, encouraged by the Law Society's recommendations on methods of practice, is to try and be as helpful and informative as possible, which indeed Dodds & Son had been.

FENCES AND BOUNDARIES

The first question on the form concerned the ownership of walls, fences, hedges and ditches; the answer referred to a plan, included with the replies, which was drawn at the time the house was first built. Where a line on a plan indicates a boundary between two properties it is common practice to show a T mark on one side of the line. This means that the particular fence or hedge belongs to the owner of the property inside which the T mark appears. By referring to the plan on which the T marks were drawn in, Matthew could tell which fences were his and which were his neighbour's. Although two of the fences appeared to belong to 14 Twintree Avenue, there was nothing to say that he was obliged to maintain them. Sometimes there is a covenant to maintain boundary fences but there was none in this case. This means that Matthew could not be forced to maintain his fences, but the same applied to his neighbour.

If no definite evidence exists as to ownership of boundaries, then certain presumptions apply. The Land Registry filed plan indicates general boundaries only (unless noted as fixed) and cannot be used in boundary disputes. With fences, the presumption is that a wooden fence belongs to the owner of the land on the side where the supporting posts are. If there is a ditch and then a hedge on your land, you own the land up to the hedge, because it is presumed that a person cannot cut a ditch in another man's land.

DISPUTES AND GUARANTEES

Question 2 was about disputes, of which the replies said that there were none. This is an important question to a buyer because you do not want to buy a house and find yourself involved in a legal wrangle with your neighbours.

Question 3 related to notices; again there were none.

Then followed a question about guarantees. This referred to such things as the certificate issued by the National House-Building Council for houses built under their scheme, or woodworm treatment guarantees, or agreements relating to roads or a footpath. (This would apply more to a house in a new development, but even for a second-hand house which abuts a private road, there may be an agreement with neighbouring proprietors as to maintenance.) A buyer should be concerned to get the benefit of any such guarantees. Information is requested now about them, so that on completion they can be transferred to the newcomer. This can be by a simple letter from the seller to the buyer saying 'In consideration of your completing the purchase of my house, I now assign to you the benefit of the guarantee dated XYZ which I received from AB regarding CD and E.' A copy of the letter of assignment should be sent to the people who gave the guarantee.

Then followed three questions about gas, electricity, drainage and other main services (they were connected) and whether any exclusive or shared facilities affected the property.

OVERRIDING INTERESTS
Question 8 on the form asked Mr Timms to disclose whether there were any adverse rights affecting the house. This is a very important question for all buyers to ask and its relevance will become clear if we look at what is meant by an 'overriding interest', mentioned in para C of question 8. Overriding interests comprise a major category of interest in registered land. Basically, they are third-party interests which bind a buyer of registered land notwithstanding that they are not recorded on the register and notwithstanding that the buyer has no actual knowledge of their existence. They are an exception to the basic principle of registered land, that all matters relevant to title are shown on the register. The justification for this seems to be that overriding interests, in the main, are rights which any buyer can easily discover if he bothers to go and look at the property he is intending to buy.

A list of overriding interests is contained in section 70(1) of the Land Registration Act 1925. The most important ones likely to affect a buyer are squatters' rights, informal rights of way and similar rights, leases of under 21 years (which are not capable of being registered) and the 'rights of every person in actual occupation'.

One point to remember, as a buyer of registered land, is that you do not become the legal owner of the property until your name is entered as registered proprietor on the proprietorship register by the Land Registry. This usually happens about one month after the property is transferred to you on completion. Thus, there is the added danger of a binding overriding interest arising (for example a lease of under 21 years) in between the date of the actual transfer to you and being registered as the new registered proprietor. The need, therefore, for a buyer to make careful enquiries and a close inspection of the property he is intending to buy cannot be overstressed.

Looking at question 8 in more detail, question 8(A) asks if there are any rights of way or rights of a similar nature affecting the property. Where there is someone else, beside the seller, living on the property, if that person also has any interest or rights in the property, by contributing towards the purchase price for instance, that interest will bind a buyer as an overriding interest even after he has bought the property, unless when he made enquiries about the rights of such a person they were not disclosed. The most likely persons to have such an interest are the seller's wife or other members of the family.

If you discover that there is such a person living on the property you are entitled to ask that he or she sign a declaration along the following lines before contracts are exchanged.

're:

In consideration of (seller) and (buyer) entering into a contract with each other for the sale and purchase with vacant possession of the property known as . . . I, AB undertake that from the date of payment to (seller) of all the purchase money due under the contract, I shall not seek to enforce against (buyer) or his successors in title any right that I may have or may in the future have in the property, so that (buyer) and his successors in title shall from the date of payment enjoy the property free from all claims or rights that I may have or may in the future have.

Dated

Signed AB'

Alternatively, you may insist that the seller's solicitor obtain that person's signature to the contract, to show that he or she agrees to the sale; he or she cannot then assert any rights to the property.

Finally, paragraph C asks if there are any other types of overriding interests affecting the property.

Luckily for Matthew, Mr Timms was a widower without any family and Dodds & Son assured him that there were no other adverse interests affecting the house. Certainly Matthew had not noticed anyone other than Mr Timms on the property when he had first seen it, but he decided that he would call again on Mr Timms before exchange of contracts, just to make sure.

OTHER QUESTIONS

Question 9 was about restrictions and he was told that, so far as the seller knew, all the restrictive covenants had been complied with and that any consents required by any covenants had been obtained.

Question 10 was a multiple question dealing with planning. Paragraph A asked since when the property had had its present use, and whether that use was continuous. The reply confirmed that the property had been continuously used, since 1960, as a private dwelling house. This was consistent with clause D of the special conditions of sale in the draft contract. Paragraph B asked whether any building work or alterations had been carried out on the property in the previous four years. If building work has been carried out on a property in breach of planning control, the local authority can take enforcement proceedings (for example to pull down a garage); but where more than four years elapses from when the breach occurred (that is when the work was done) then the local authority loses the right to take any further action. The reply assured Matthew that no buildings had been erected nor alterations made to the house in the past four years, and since the house was originally built in 1960 there was no need for him to investigate the planning consent that had then been given.

The next question dealt with fixtures and fittings. Where an object is so attached to property as to become part of it, it is called a fixture and passes automatically to a buyer of the property unless specifically excluded from the sale. Examples of fixtures are a boiler cemented to the floor, fixed partitions, radiators in a central heating system. However, there are always some marginal items, light fittings, greenhouses, television aerials, fitted cupboards, trees and roses, and so on, which might or might not be fixtures – if not, the seller is entitled to remove them. By asking the seller which of these items he intends to take with him, later disputes are, hopefully, avoided.

Question 12 asked for the rateable value of the property and whether any work had been carried out which might increase this.

The next question asked about completion and when vacant possession would be given. The answer was four weeks after exchange of contracts. Matthew had crossed out questions 14 (which concerns developers only) and 15 (new properties). In reply to Matthew's additional enquiry regarding the restrictive covenants to Minford Estates Developments Ltd, Dodds & Son had written 'Please see reply to enquiry 9', which confirmed that all was well.

Matthew was satisfied with the answers he had received to his preliminary enquiries. He was now ready to move onto the next stage.

approval of draft contract

Matthew was now ready to return the draft contract, approved by him subject to the addition of a special condition of sale specifying that the curtains and fitted carpets in the house were included in the purchase price.

The custom between solicitors is that amendments to draft documents should appear in various coloured inks, red first, then green and so on. However, in the case of contracts for the sale of residential property most solicitors negotiate the terms of the contract by correspondence headed 'subject to contract'. Where alterations are minimal, as is probable in the case of a house with registered title, the buyer should return the document unmarked (courtesy and tradition demand that he return the top copy not the carbon), so that it can be used for signature by the seller without retyping, together with a covering letter stating that he approves the draft contract subject to his proposed amendment. If this amendment is approved by the seller's solicitor, the buyer can incorporate it in the carbon copy he has retained and use this for signature on his part.

Matthew therefore returned the top copy of the draft contract to Dodds & Son with following covering letter:

38 Broadstone Drive
Hastings, Sussex

18th January 1983

To: Messrs Dodds & Son

Dear Sirs,

Re: 14 Twintree Avenue, Minford

Thank you for your letter of 17th January. I now return the draft contract which I approve, subject to satisfactory local searches and survey, and subject to the addition of the following special condition: 'The curtains and fitted carpets at present on the property are to be included in the purchase price'. When I have received back my local searches and heard from my proposed mortgagees, I shall be ready to exchange contracts.

I have discussed with your client the question of completion: we have provisionally agreed that I shall be able to move in on tuesday, 1st March.

Yours faithfully,

M. J. Seaton

The second paragraph of this letter referred to a telephone conversation which Mr Timms had had with Matthew on the question of moving day. Matthew estimated that they would need about five more weeks to deal with various formalities. On that basis, 1st March was not too optimistic.

replies to local searches

At the end of the week, Matthew received his local search certificate and replies to the enquiries he had made of Minford District Council on form LLC1.

The local search certificate revealed that there was one registration affecting 14 Twintree Avenue at the date of the certificate. The 'attached schedule' described this entry as being that the property was in a smoke control zone (which was quite normal for the area).

The replies to the enquiries made on form Con 29A were also satisfactory. Minford DC had supplied the answers on a standard printed sheet. These revealed that Twintree Avenue was maintainable at public expense; that there were no present proposals for road widening or for constructing any major roads in the area; that there were no repair, sanitary or other similar notices on the property; that the property was drained into a public sewer; that the property was not in an area liable to be compulsorily acquired; and that the local plan for the district showed the area as zoned primarily for residential use. From the reply to his additional enquiry, he discovered that there were no pipe-lines in close proximity to the house. Also, there were no enforcement proceedings being taken for breach of planning control.

If there are enforcement proceedings, the answers to the local authority enquiries will show the number and date of the enforcement notice, and the planning regulation that has been breached, for example 'Enforcement notice No. FN1234 dated 16 December 1982; breach of condition 4 on planning permission No. 1764'. The buyer should ask the seller or seller's solicitor for a copy of the notice, but can also go to the planning department of the local authority, who will find the notice and give the buyer the details.

Matthew heaved a sigh of relief. A colleague of his who was also doing her own conveyancing had recently discovered, from her enquiries of the district council, that there was an enforcement notice against the house she was hoping to buy. By inspecting the register of enforcement proceedings, kept by the district planning office, the colleague had found out that her seller had built a garage a few months previously, which did not conform to the specifications laid down in the planning permission. She was presently involved in negotiations with the other side for an assurance from the seller that the necessary work would be carried out to make the garage conform to the specifications before completion (a special condition of sale to be included in the draft contract to this effect). Alternatively, she could have asked that the purchase price be reduced, so that she could have the work done after completion without being out of pocket.

If you find anything on your searches which cannot be resolved by clarification by the local authority and/or subsequent negotiation with the other side, such as a proposal for compulsory acquisition, you should look for another property or consult a solicitor.

mortgage offer

That same friday, Matthew received a letter from the Forthright Building Society

FORTHRIGHT BUILDING SOCIETY

88 Lomax Street
Minford, Surrey

20th January 1983

To: M. J. Seaton Esq

Dear Sir,

Re: 14 Twintree Avenue, Minford

The society has now received the report of its surveyor regarding the above property and is able to offer you an advance in the sum of £32,000 to be secured on a mortgage of the above property. The loan is conditional upon its being taken up within three months of this date.

I enclose details of the proposed loan on our formal notification, from which you will see that the interest rate will be 11% per annum at first, but the society reserves the right to alter the interest rate on giving notice.
The loan will be repayable over a 25 year period by monthly instalments of £317.

The solicitors who will act for the society in connection with the legal formalities of the mortgage will be Messrs Hodgson, Green & Co, of this town, who will be getting in touch with you shortly.

Yours faithfully,

M. C. Templeton
Manager

The enclosed notification and acceptance form was in these terms:

Head office:
Forthright House,
Somerset Square,
London EC3

please reply to:
88 Lomax Street
Minford, Surrey

20th January 1983

To: Matthew J. Seaton Esq

Offer of advance

<u>Re: 14 Twintree Avenue, Minford</u>

Forthright Building Society offers to advance you the sum mentioned below, such sum to be secured on the above property, upon these terms and conditions:

1. The property is freehold/~~leasehold with ..... years to run.~~
2. The offer is subject to the society being finally satisfied as to your financial position and prospects.
3. Amount to be advanced £32,000 repayable by monthly payments of £317 each over a period of 25 years. Each payment includes a proportion of principal and of interest.
4. Interest rate 11 per centum per annum. The right is reserved to vary this rate of interest on giving notice to do so. Effect may be given to variations of the interest rate by increasing or decreasing the period over which payments are made (see para 3 above).
5. The property must throughout the period of the loan remain insured against fire and other risks in a sum of not less than its full value; this at first is £40,000. The insurance will be arranged with a company approved by the society.
6. The legal formalities in connection with the mortgage will be dealt with on behalf of the society by the society's solicitors Messrs Hodgson, Green & Co of 67 Lomax Street, Minford, Surrey. Their fees and disbursements are payable by you and are deducted from the loan when it is made. The loan is conditional upon the society's solicitors being satisfied regarding the property's title and otherwise.
7. ~~The repairs listed in the accompanying schedule must be effected before completion/within months of completion.~~
8. The property must not be let in any way nor may alterations or additions be made to it without the society's written consent, to be obtained in advance.
9. The society reserves the right to modify or withdraw this offer at any time until the loan is effected.

G. Percy Marshall
Advance Manager

Most building societies include a further requirement in their offers of advance, as a result of a recent decision by the House of Lords. The decision suggests that a wife, co-habitor, parent or other person living in a property may have, or have acquired, rights in the property even though it is not in that person's name. The building societies therefore ask that all people likely to be living in the property should sign a separate undertaking, that they will not exert their right (if any) to stay on in the house if the owner should fail to repay the loan and the society has to sell the property to recover its debt. Matthew's wife Emma would have to sign such an undertaking, usually called a form of consent. This was why Matthew had been asked to list intended occupants when he first applied for an advance from the Forthright Building Society.

If you have applied to a bank for an advance under their home loan scheme, the offer you will receive will be in similar terms to the Forthright's one. The bank will probably require an undertaking in the form of a 'deed of postponement' rather than a form of consent.

An advance of £32,000 was what Matthew had applied for and this had been granted. It is quite normal to find that a loan has to be taken up within a set number of months, otherwise the offer to lend the money lapses. In practice, a building society is often willing to extend the time limit if the delay is explained.

It is also quite normal for the borrower to have to pay the legal costs of the building society's solicitors. In this case it was probable that Hodgson, Green & Co acted generally for the Minford branch of the building society. Some building societies, particularly the larger ones, adopt a panel system, whereby many solicitors all over the country are on a panel of solicitors who can act for them. In this way it often happens that the same solicitor acts for the buyer and for the building society, with a saving in legal fees to the buyer as a result. Alternatively, the building society may instruct the buyer's solicitor, if he has one, to act for them.

Clause 8 showed that, strictly speaking, no lettings or alterations could be made without the building society's consent.

IT IS ONLY AN OFFER

There was nothing binding, either on the building society or on Matthew, about the offer of a mortgage: clause 9 of the official notification made this clear. A building society rarely commits itself in advance to making a loan so that, theoretically at least, the buyer of a house may be placed in a vulnerable position. He has to commit himself to the seller by a binding contract on the strength of an offer from a building society, which is not binding, to lend him part of the purchase price. If for some reason, such as the buyer's financial circumstances taking a turn for the worse, the building society were to back out before the loan was made, or in an economic crisis the proposed interest rate was increased, the buyer could do nothing about it.

The form from the Forthright Building Society was in duplicate, an original and a tear-off copy. A notice on the back of the form said that the society did not warrant that the purchase price was reasonable, nor that the house was fit for human habitation. This was a formality, quite usual, nowadays, which the society put in to cover itself on these questions.

The terms of the offer were as Matthew had expected. He had, in fact, worked out what his monthly payments would be, with the help of the calculation tables in *Raising the money to buy your home*. He felt able to sign the form of acceptance. (Since the introduction of mortgage interest relief at source (MIRAS) in April 1983, basic rate taxpayers with a mortgage not exceeding £30,000 make their repayments net of tax rather than tax relief being allowed on their salary via PAYE coding.)

ACCEPTANCE

21st January 1983

To: Forthright Building Society

I, *Matthew J. Seaton of 38 Broadstone Drive, Hastings, Sussex* accept your offer to make an advance to be secured on *14 Twintree Avenue, Minford, Surrey,* upon the terms and conditions made known to me.

My solicitors are ....

signed *M. J. Seaton*

The acceptance, which Matthew had to sign and return to the society was appended to the bottom of the copy. He sent the following letter with it:

38 Broadstone Drive
Hastings, Sussex

21st January 1983

To: The Manager,
Forthright Building Society,
Minford, Surrey

Dear Sir,

Re: 14 Twintree Avenue, Minford

Thank you for your letter of 20th January and its enclosure, from which I am pleased to learn that you are willing to grant me a mortgage loan to be secured on the above. I note the terms of the advance, and look forward to hearing from your solicitors. I return the acceptance form, duly signed by me.

Yours faithfully,

M. J. Seaton

Matthew had not yet heard from Andrew Robertson & Co with their report on the survey they had carried out for him. He knew from the society's letter of 20th January that they had inspected the property. He telephoned Mr James Robertson, who informed him that his report was in draft and he would be receiving it shortly.

the amended draft contract

The third piece of correspondence Matthew received that day was a letter from Dodds & Son.

DODDS & SON
Solicitors

1 Charter Street
Minford, Surrey

20th January 1983

To: M. J. Seaton Esq

Dear Sir,

Re: 14 Twintree Avenue, Minford

We thank you for your letter of 18th January, returning the draft contract. We approve your suggested amendment which we have included as Clause G in the special conditions of sale. We are treating the top copy as an engrossment of the contract.

We are obtaining our client's signature to the contract and on receipt of the part signed by you and the balance of the deposit, we shall let you have the part signed by the vendor and the balance of the title. We confirm that the completion date should be 1st March 1983, and have inserted that date in the contract.

Yours faithfully,
Dodds & Son

When the wording of a contract is agreed, each side prepares a fair copy of it which is called an engrossment. If the contract is approved as originally drafted, or with minor variations, each side uses their copy of the draft contract as the engrossment itself. The seller then signs the engrossed contract held by his solicitor and the buyer signs the one held by him or his solicitor. As will happen in Matthew's case a little later on, the contract is made by the parties 'swopping' their signed contracts.

Matthew would ask one of the secretaries at the school if she would kindly type the new clause G in the copy of the draft contract form he had retained, so that he could use it as his engrossment.

insurance

One further matter a buyer should attend to before exchange of contracts is insurance.

Once contracts are exchanged, the risk in the property passes to the buyer and the seller is under no duty to maintain any insurance on it. Both the Law Society's and National conditions of sale state this clearly in condition 11 and condition 21 respectively. Thus if, for example, the property was flooded between exchange of contracts and completion, the buyer would still have to go through with the purchase and bear the cost of repairs. So the insurance of the property you are buying should start from the moment you exchange contracts.

A buyer should insure the property for risks such as fire, storm, flood, damage by burglars and to cover the owner's liability for accidents to third parties caused by the state of the property – a roof-tile falling down and injuring someone, for instance. A building policy covers these risks. Eventually, Matthew would need a policy that covers contents as well as building.

TAKING OVER THE SELLER'S?
It may be possible to take over the seller's existing policy, but the more common practice today (except in the case of leasehold property, when it may be better to take over a policy which complies with the lease) is to take out a new one.

If you are taking over an existing policy, the reply to question 4 on the *Enquiries before contract* form should give you details of the policy. You can then write to the insurance company and advise them of your interest in the property. On completion, you would have to pay back to the seller a proportionate part of the premium he has paid. After completion, the policy would have to be sent to the insurance company so that your interest and that of your mortgagee (if any) can be formally noted on the policy and in their records. If you so wish, you can, of course, increase the cover.

It is, however, generally much better to take out a new policy, especially since the property may well be underinsured. If you already have an insurance company with which you are satisfied, get a proposal form for a household building policy and ask for cover to start immediately contracts have been exchanged; then inform your company when this has happened and pay the first premium.

WHEN THERE IS A MORTGAGE

If, as in Matthew's case, you are obtaining a loan from a building society, the society will almost certainly suggest that you insure through an insurance company it knows well. A building society obviously has a strong vested interest in the insurance: if the property were to burn down, uninsured, most of their security would have gone up in smoke. The insurance policy will have a note of the mortgage endorsed on it.

On Matthew's application form from the Forthright Building Society, there had been a section about insurance. Normally a borrower is entitled to choose from three named insurance companies. The manager of the society had suggested the Bridstow Insurance Company Ltd which had a local office nearby, and Matthew had agreed. Matthew did not have to fill in a proposal form himself, the matter was completely handled by the society. Where a building society insures its borrowers' property through a special block policy with the insurance company, the borrower will not get a copy of the insurance policy. He should, however, make sure to get all the relevant details from the society.

A building society often pays the first premium to make sure that the insurance is effective and deducts the amount from the loan to the buyer. Similarly, some building societies also pay the subsequent insurance premiums and add the amount each year to one of the monthly mortgage payments. Eventually the Forthright would notify Matthew how much his premium was.

Whether you yourself take out the insurance or the building society does, check that the sum insured is adequate to cover the cost of wholly rebuilding the property, after allowing for architects' and surveyors' fees and the cost of clearing the site of debris, in the case of total destruction.

There can be quite a difference between the market value of a house and its reinstatement value. This is always higher than the market value and it is on this amount that a building society takes out insurance, not on the amount of the market value or amount of the mortgage loan.

It is quite likely that the building society will look after a building policy only, so the buyer should make sure that contents insurance starts as soon as there is any of his own property inside the house. This may be before moving day, if there is an agreement between the seller and buyer that certain items will be left inside the house. It is sensible to take out a house contents policy with the same company as the building is insured with.

the building society's solicitors

After the weekend, Matthew heard from the solicitors acting for the Forthright Building Society.

HODGSON, GREEN & CO
Solicitors   *67 Lomax Street*
Minford, Surrey

21st January 1983

To: Matthew J. Seaton Esq

Dear Sir,

Re: 14 Twintree Avenue, Minford

Our clients Forthright Building Society have instructed us with regard to an advance on mortgage of £32,000 to be made to you and to be secured on the above property. We understand that you will be acting for yourself in this matter.

When the legal formalities regarding your purchase are sufficiently advanced, please let us have the following documents: contract, Preliminary Enquiries and replies, local searches, office copies of the entries on the Register and filed plan, authority for us to inspect the Register, Requisitions on Title and replies and draft Transfer as approved by the vendor's solicitors.

Yours faithfully,
Hodgson, Green & Co

This was just the normal introductory letter. Apart from a routine acknowledgment, no further action was needed with Hodgson, Green & Co until after exchange of contracts. If there had been anything that might worry the building society solicitors (for instance, a possible breach of restrictive covenant or evidence of a boundary dispute), Matthew should have written immediately to Hodgson, Green & Co, and not waited until after exchange of contracts. Otherwise there would have been a risk of the building society withdrawing their mortgage offer after Matthew had already committed himself to the purchase by exchanging contracts.

visit to the local authority

The local search and enquiries had given Matthew information of a public nature directly relevant to 14 Twintree Avenue. However, he and Emma planned to make Minford their home for several years and he wanted to know more about the probable future development of Minford and the surrounding area. He had the afternoon free from school and decided that he would go to Guildford to look at the structure plan for the whole area which was kept at Surrey County Council planning offices. Then he would go to Minford to see the local plan kept by Minford District Council planning authority.

Both structure and local plans are prepared by the local planning authority and are submitted to the Secretary of State for his approval. A structure plan is really a 'policy' plan, containing big scale plans for an area for the next 5 to 7 years. How far these plans materialise depends largely on the availability of finance. It gives information on general matters such as projected population numbers, traffic policies, education policy, estimated growth of office space, and restrictions on the total number of houses that can be built in the area. A local plan, on the other hand, gives more detailed information on current plans for a specific area, for example the site for a new school and the location of actual street clearance.

Matthew found the people in both planning offices extremely helpful and willing to explain the meaning of the plans to him. As far as he could judge, nothing that was planned was likely to affect 14 Twintree Avenue adversely.

While he was at the district council planning offices, he called in on the highways department to see if there were any new road proposals or traffic schemes for Minford. His local searches had confirmed that there were no proposed roads within 200 metres of the house, but anything farther than that would not be disclosed on the search.

Finally, he asked to see the register of planning applications made for 14 Twintree Avenue. This showed that planning permission had been given to Minford Estate Developments Ltd in 1958 to build the estate of houses which now included 14 Twintree Avenue. By looking at the plans for the estate which the council had approved, Matthew was able to identify 14 Twintree Avenue and to check that the house built was the same as that for which permission had been given. He came away with a much better idea about the locality, present and future.

looking at the house
Matthew knew that he would probably be in a position to exchange contracts with Mr Timms within the next few days so, as he was in Minford, he telephoned Mr Timms to ask if he could visit the house. It is always

advisable to compare the description of the property in the contract and the plan with the actual property to ensure that they correspond. (If they do not, you should raise the question with the seller and if necessary consult a solicitor.) And it is important for a buyer to make a thorough inspection of the property before exchanging contracts. Matthew had with him the copy of the filed plan Dodds & Son had sent him. He compared the plan with the actual property to see whether the plan was correct. He also saw that there was nothing on the property which could be the cause of confusion or disputes with neighbours in the future, such as a row of trees near the boundary of a garden.

Matthew was especially careful to check that there was no-one other than Mr Timms in the house or outside in the garden. If he had found someone there, he would have asked them their reason for being on the property and if necessary whether they had any interest in it. If they had, he would have asked Dodds & Son to obtain their signature to the contract or an undertaking in similar form to that given on page 46.

the surveyor's report
Matthew's surveyor's report arrived the following morning. It was written in typical surveyors language but basically told him that the house was structurally sound, though full of petty faults which were largely design errors and could not now be rectified. There were a couple of loose tiles on the roof and some cracks needed making good. Apart from this, the house was in good order. There was nothing in the surveyor's report to deter Matthew from buying the house or to justify his asking for a reduction in the purchase price.

He decided it was time to think about contents insurance and wrote to the Bridstow Insurance Co, requesting a proposal form for contents insurance on the house. He decided that he would not insure the contents until his own furniture and belongings were moved in on March 1st. He would take a chance on the curtains and carpets Mr Timms was leaving behind.

exchange of contracts

A contract for the sale and purchase of a house only becomes legally binding on the parties once 'an exchange of contracts' has taken place. The contract really consists of two identical documents and an 'exchange of contracts' is when one party (or his solicitor), having received the other party's signed contract, posts his signed contract to the other party (or to his solicitor).

By tradition, it is the buyer who sends his contract first. If your purchase is not dependent on the sale of your present, or some other, property, you can send off your signed contract as soon as you have completed your searches and enquiries, received your survey report and mortgage offer and inspected the property.

The procedure is that you send off your signed contract with a cheque for the whole or balance of the deposit. When it is received by the seller's solicitor, he will date both parts, insert the completion date into both parts (unless that has already been done), and send the seller's signed contract back to you. Contracts are now exchanged. In cases of dispute, contracts are deemed to be exchanged when the seller's solicitor commits the seller's signed contract to the post. Remember that if the contract incorporates the Law Society's general conditions of sale, you will need a banker's draft for the deposit.

Occasionally, if both sides live in the same town, exchange of contracts is done in person, usually at the seller's solicitor's office. Exactly the same procedure is followed; the date of exchange will be the date of the meeting.

IF THERE IS A CHAIN
Problems of timing involved in chain transactions have led to the growth of a new practice among solicitors of 'exchange of contracts by telephone'. However, the practice is still fraught with uncertainties and it is not recommended that a buyer acting without a solicitor attempt such an exchange.

If your purchase is dependent on the sale of your present or other property, it is obvious that you should receive your buyer's signed purchase contract and his deposit before you send your signed contract and deposit to your seller's solicitor.

PROBLEMS WITH THE DEPOSIT
A buyer may have difficulty in finding the ready cash to pay the 10 per cent deposit, especially if he is selling his present home and buying another. Here a bank bridging loan can prove useful, although expensive. A bank will make a bridging loan to a buyer for the amount of the deposit, but only after contracts for the sale of his present home have actually been exchanged. Long experience has taught banks to be chary of a seller's hopes. A bank will usually require an undertaking from the buyer's

solicitor that when he receives the sale monies (from the property his client is selling), he will retain sufficient to repay the bridging loan for the purchase deposit for the house his client is buying. If you are doing your own conveyancing, the solicitor of the buyer of your present home will probably consent to giving such an undertaking to your bank, on payment of a small fee. Or a deposit could be passed from your buyer's solicitor to the one of the person from whom you are buying, thus 'leapfrogging' you and avoiding the problem of a solicitor not being willing to hand a deposit to a non-solicitor.

But if you are a first time buyer with the aid of a 95 or 100 per cent mortgage from a building society and you need bridging finance to pay the deposit, there is a risk that your efforts to do your own conveyancing may have to end. Whereas a bridging loan for the deposit can sometimes be arranged with the help of the building society's or your own buyer's solicitors, it would seem that for a first time, 100 per cent mortgage buyer doing his own conveyancing there is little hope of obtaining institutional finance additional to his mortgage. If you have no private means of paying the deposit (perhaps a relative will help) you may have to hand your conveyancing over to a solicitor.

MATTHEW'S EXCHANGE
Matthew was now ready to send his signed contract to buy 14 Twintree Avenue and a cheque for the balance of the deposit to Dodds & Son. This was because
○ the form and wording of the contract had been agreed
○ the replies he had received to his enquiries before contract had been satisfactory
○ the local search certificate and replies to enquiries made of the local authority were satisfactory
○ he had made arrangements to borrow on mortgage the amount he needed
○ arrangements had been made for the property to be insured
○ he had received a satisfactory report from a surveyor
○ he had made a satisfactory inspection of the property
○ he had the necessary finance for the deposit.
He therefore sent his signed contract to Dodds & Son with this letter:

38 Broadstone Drive
Hastings, Sussex

26th January 1983

To: Messrs Dodds & Son

Dear Sirs,

Re: 14 Twintree Avenue

I now enclose the contract signed by me. Please date it. I have inserted 1st March as the date for completion, as agreed with Mr Timms.

Flint & Morgan hold a preliminary deposit of £100 and I now enclose my cheque for £3,900, the balance of the deposit. I look forward to receiving from you as soon as possible the contract signed by your client and an authority to inspect the register.

Yours faithfully,

M. J. Seaton

Matthew heard from the Bridstow Insurance Co Ltd, sending him a proposal form for house contents insurance and soon afterwards from Dodds & Son.

DODDS & SON
Solicitors

1 Charter Street
Minford, Surrey

27th January 1983

To: M. J. Seaton Esq

Dear Sir,

Re: 14 Twintree Avenue, Minford

We thank you for your letter of yesterday enclosing contract duly signed and cheque for £3,900 in our favour being balance of deposit, receipt of which in the capacity of stakeholders we hereby acknowledge.

We now have pleasure in enclosing contract signed by our client Mr Timms. We have dated both parts of the contract with to-day's date and confirm that the date for completion is fixed by the contract at 1st March 1983. We enclose an authority to inspect the register to complete the delivery of title.

We await your requisitions on title and draft transfer for approval in due course.

Yours faithfully,
Dodds & Son

As contracts had now been exchanged and had become legally binding on both parties, Matthew telephoned the Forthright Building Society to ask them to effect immediate insurance cover and sent a confirmatory letter.

the seller's title

Before exchange of contracts, a buyer's work consists mainly in checking various things about the property; his post-contract work consists of investigating the seller's title, getting the ownership of the property transferred to him, obtaining his mortgage finance and paying the purchase price to the seller. In the case of registered property, the Land Registry has fortunately taken away practically all the post-contract work, leaving just a few formalities to be attended to.

After exchange of contracts, the seller's solicitor must prove the seller's ownership of the property, and that it can be properly transferred to the buyer. He does this by supplying the buyer or his solicitor with office copies of the entries on the register and filed plan (if he has not already done so) and an authority to inspect the register. Most sellers' solicitors send a full set of office copies to the buyer with the draft contract (a practice encouraged by the Law Society), so that all you will receive after the contract is made is an authority to inspect the register.

Office copies bear the date on which they were issued by the Land Registry, and show the state of the register at that date. However, a buyer must ensure that there has been no change in the register between the date of the issue of the office copies and the date on which he completes his purchase. To do this, he will make another search of the register a short time before completion. The certificate of search he receives back from the Land Registry would reveal any such change.

But the register is private; it is not open to public inspection. Hence the authority to inspect the register, which is the seller's written permission for the buyer to inspect the register, and which the buyer must send to the Land Registry with his application for an official search.

Matthew had already studied carefully the office copies of the entries on the register and the filed plan of 14 Twintree Avenue which Dodds & Son had sent him with the draft contract. He was satisfied that the description of the property in the property register and the filed plan corresponded with that which he was buying and that Mr Timms was the registered proprietor with title absolute. He had noted the implications of the restrictive covenants in favour of Minford Estate Developments Ltd entered on the charges register of the property, and that the house was subject to an existing mortgage in favour of Minford Building Society, which would have to be discharged on completion.

He took out the office copies from his file; he was now ready to make his requisitions on title.

cautions, notices, restrictions and inhibitions

Up until now we have assumed that everything about the seller's title is normal. But occasionally something may appear on the register which makes the buying process a little more difficult.

Within the system of registration of title, there is a procedure for anyone claiming an interest in the house, perhaps under a previous contract which the seller has repudiated, to register a 'caution' or a 'notice' on the register. If you discover a caution on your office copy entries, or later on your official certificate of search, you should not complete your purchase unless the person who registered the caution (his name appears on the register) signs a statement saying that he withdraws it. Generally speaking, a notice protects an interest of which you are already aware and are willing to take the property subject to, for example a right of way. If this is not the case, or if the notice protects the right of a wife or husband of the seller (who is not a joint proprietor) to remain in the property, you will need the person who entered the notice to sign a release of his or her rights in the property, before completion. On the whole, the likelihood of a caution or notice appearing on a normal house-seller's title is rare.

Examples of restrictions and inhibitions on the proprietorship register were given earlier (page 32). Unfortunately, the Land Registry has a habit of registering under these headings purely routine items which are of no concern to a buyer. How do you find out whether an entry is the one that affects you or the 99 you can ignore? It is a little publicised fact that every district land registry has an excellent enquiry department that will answer reasonable enquiries about registered property from solicitors or members of the public. Furthermore, each district land registry has a number of qualified legal employees on the staff who can be consulted if necessary. So when faced with such a problem, telephone or visit the experts.

requisitions on title: buyer to seller

Requisitions on title are additional questions about the property. Most buyers' solicitors make standard enquiries on a printed form of requisitions, form Con 28B *Requisitions on title*. The form incorporates, by reference, the preliminary enquiries made before exchange of contracts, so shortening the list of enquiries that have to be made. (In the rare case of no preliminary enquiries having been made, a 'long' version of this form is available from Oyez).

Certain questions on the form should be deleted if they are irrelevant, such as those which relate to leaseholds when you are buying a freehold. Matthew crossed out question 2(B) (dealing with rent and insurance) and question 6 (dealing with notification about the sale of the property) because these are only relevant to leasehold property. He also crossed out question 3 part of which applies to unregistered land and the other part (which does apply to registered land) has only to be asked where no office copy of the entries on the register has been supplied and where the land certificate is on deposit at the Land Registry, which as a rule happens only where one property is being sold off from an estate or block of properties.

This left question 1 which asked for confirmation that the answers given to the enquiries before contract were still valid. If not, details of any changes were asked for.

Question 2(A) asked for receipts for rates and other outgoings to be produced and arrears allowed for and 2(C) asked for a completion statement, which tells the buyer exactly what he will have to pay on completion.

Question 4 referred to mortgages and required that proof would have to be given that Mr Timms' mortgage had been paid off and asked how this would be done. Where the title of property is registered, it is common for a Land Registry form (53(Co)) to be used by the building society for discharging a mortgage. The Land Registry then cancels the entries on the register relating to the mortgage. But for some strange reason, building societies (and other lenders) often find it difficult to arrange for form 53(Co) to be ready at completion, and instead the seller's solicitor hands over an undertaking to provide it within so-many days. The question asked whether form 53(Co) would be used on completion or an undertaking, and if the latter, what it would say.

Question 5(A)(i) states that vacant possession must be given on completion. 5(A)(ii) concerns the problem of an overriding interest, discussed earlier on page 46. It asks whether every person living in the property has agreed to leave on or before completion, the aim of the question being to ensure that the buyer will not be saddled with the interests or claims of such persons. The reply to this question will help a buyer to decide whether to insist on his right to go into possession of the property on or immediately before completion, so that when the property is actually transferred to him, he is the only one on the property. This right is provided for in condition 5(4) of the National Conditions of Sale. There is no equivalent provision in the Law Society general conditions.

Question 5(A)(iii) then asked what arrangements were to be made about handing over the keys. 5(B) being applicable only to property subject to an existing tenancy, Matthew crossed it out.

Finally question 7 asked where completion would take place, or if it could be by post, and about payment.

There is extra space on the form for making additional requisitions, applicable to the particular sale in question. Matthew added: 'Please supply an additional authority to inspect the register, addressed to Hodgson, Green & Co of 67 Lomax Street, Minford who act for my intended mortgagees.' The necessity for this arose from what Hodgson, Green & Co had said in their letter to Matthew of 21st January. Among the items they had asked to receive was an 'authority for us to inspect the register'. This implied that although Matthew would be making his official search of the register just before completion, Hodgson, Green & Co wanted to make one, too, on behalf of the Forthright Building Society. They, too, had to be sure that there had been no change to the register since the date of the office copies.

Both the National and Law Society conditions of sale impose time limits on the making of requisitions, and for this purpse time is of the essence. This means that the buyer has to deliver his requisitions to the seller within the specified time, otherwise the seller can refuse to answer them (in practice, this is unusual) and the buyer has to accept the seller's title. Under the National Conditions, the requisitions must be made within 11 working days of the receipt of the office copy entries or of the date of the contract, whichever is the later. If your contract incorporates the Law Society general conditions, you have only six working days. Under the National Conditions, the seller's solicitor merely has to reply within a reasonable time, but under the Law Society ones he must reply within four working days of receiving the requisitions.

Matthew signed and dated the form of requisitions on title and sent it to Dodds & Son, together with an extra copy for their file.

the transfer

At the same time as preparing his requisitions on title, Matthew also prepared the draft transfer. This is the document which, when signed, sealed and delivered by the seller, legally transfers ownership of the house.

Of all the forms a buyer encounters, the transfer form is probably the easiest to fill in. Where the transfer is of the whole of registered property (that is, where the title number covers just the one property and it is that property which is being sold) you should use form 19 *Transfer of whole*. If you are buying the property in the joint names of yourself and your husband or wife, or some other person, use form 19(JP). Where only part of the registered property is being transferred (say one house out of ten), form 20 should be used. The forms are applicable to freehold or leasehold property.

Opposite (on page 69) is what Matthew's draft transfer looked like.

At the top of the form was a space, left blank for the time being. After completion, the Inland Revenue would emboss the appropriate stamps when the stamp duty had been paid. Also left blank for the time being were the date (hopefully 1st March would appear here) and the space where Mr Timms would sign.

Matthew used the office copy of the entries on the register to complete the form. The property register gave him the name of the county and district, a short description of the property and the title. The proprietorship register enabled him to fill in Mr Timms' full name, address and occupation. Since Mr Timms' present address was now different from that shown on the proprietorship register, he put 'formerly of 15 Chapel Lane, Minford, Surrey but now of 14 Twintree Avenue, Minford, Surrey . . .' to make the transfer tally with the register.

As Mr Timms was the actual owner as well as being the person in whom the legal title was vested, he was selling as beneficial owner (as stated in the contract). If the contract, in your case, states that the seller is selling in another capacity, that is personal representative, trustees for sale or tenant for life, the words 'beneficial owner' should be crossed out and the appropriate title inserted. Remember that if your seller is a tenant for life or trustee for sale, a receipt from at least two trustees is required (the trustees of the settlement in the case of settled land). This is achieved by making them parties to the transfer so that they 'sign, seal and deliver' the transfer in addition to the seller.

TRANSFER OF WHOLE

(Rule 98 or 115, Land Registration Rules 1925)

County and district
(or London borough)   *Surrey, Minford*

Title number.....................*SY43271604*

Property........................... *14 Twintree Avenue, Minford*

Date....................................19......... in consideration of *forty thousand* pounds (*£40,000*) the receipt whereof is hereby acknowledged I/~~We~~ *William Herbert Timms formerly of 15 Chapel Lane, Minford, Surrey, but now of 14 Twintree Avenue, Minford, Surrey, electrical engineer* ....as beneficial owner(s) hereby transfer to:

MATTHEW JOHN SEATON OF 38 BROADSTONE DRIVE, HASTINGS, SUSSEX, SCHOOLTEACHER

the land comprised in the title above mentioned.

It is hereby certified that the transaction hereby effected does not form part of a larger transaction or series of transactions in respect of which the amount or value or aggregate amount or value of the consideration exceeds *£40,000*

Signed, sealed and delivered by the said ⎤
WILLIAM HERBERT TIMMS |
in the presence of   ⎦   ....seal

Name ....
Address ....
Occupation ....

Signed, sealed and delivered by the said ⎤
.... |
in the presence of   ⎦   ....seal

Name ....
Address ....
Occupation ....

co-ownership

Matthew and his wife Emma had considered whether to put the house into their joint names. A primary reason for doing this used to be a likely saving in estate duty on the death of a joint owner. Estate duty was replaced by capital transfer tax in 1975 and does not have to be paid on what a husband leaves to his wife or vice versa.

JOINT TENANTS

Where a husband and wife (or persons in other relationships) buy a house jointly, they should agree between them what is to happen when one of them dies: will the property then go automatically to the survivor or will the dead partner's share in the house comprise part of his or her estate? Where property is to pass automatically to the survivor of two people who own a property jointly, they are said to be joint tenants. A joint tenancy is a difficult concept to explain, although easy to understand. In essence, it means that the whole interest in all of the land is vested in one and both of the joint tenants simultaneously. Neither of the joint tenants has a specific or defined interest in the property because each owns the whole, jointly with the other.

The main characteristic of a joint tenancy is that it is governed by what is called the rule of survivorship. When one of the joint tenants dies, his interest in the property automatically vests in the other, no matter what the will of the dead joint tenants says (the will is irrelevant for this purpose). The surviving joint tenant then has the whole interest in the property himself and, like any other absolute owner, has full power to deal with it as he likes, including the power to sell it, and can give to the buyer a valid receipt for the purchase money.

TENANTS IN COMMON

On the other hand, where property is held so that when one partner dies his share passes under his will or on his intestacy and not necessarily to the surviving partner, this is called a tenancy in common.

A tenant in common does have a specific share in the property, whether it be one-half, one-third or so on, and can deal with that share as he or she pleases, including leaving it by will to a third party. (The third party then becomes a tenant in common with the surviving tenant.) Because it is impossible to say, without further evidence, that on the death of one tenant in common, the survivor is entitled to the whole interest in the property, he or she cannot give a valid receipt to the buyer.

BUYING JOINTLY

The form to use if you are buying property jointly is form 19(JP), *Transfer of whole to joint proprietors*. The front of the form is exactly the same as form 19, but the back contains a declaration in this form: 'The transferees declare that the survivor of them can/cannot give a valid receipt for capital money arising on a disposition of the land.' Cross out 'cannot' if you have agreed to hold the house as joint tenants, and 'can' if you have agreed to be tenants in common.

A further difference on form 19(JP) is that there are extra attestation clauses (places for signature etc). Both buyers will have to sign the eventual transfer in addition to the seller, because they have agreed to do something (that is, hold as joint tenants or tenants in common) within the body of the deed.

getting the transfer ready

On both forms 19 and 19(JP) there is a space at the bottom of the front page for any special clauses that may have to be added, should this be necessary. Sometimes a seller's solicitor will want a clause in the transfer to the effect that the buyer will comply with the restrictive covenants and will indemnify the seller for any future liability that might arise from a breach of the covenants. The contract will tell you if such a clause is required (in the special conditions of sale) and the precise form it should take, so you can copy it from the contract into the transfer form; if you do not, the seller's solicitor will probably add it when approving the draft transfer. There is no reason why a buyer should object to such a clause and indeed few solicitors will ask for one to be included. One difference it does make is that the buyer has to sign the transfer as well as the seller; again this is because he is agreeing to do something within the body of the deed.

The only other item that Matthew had to add to his draft transfer form was the figure at the end of the certificate of value, which is there because of stamp duty. If the price of the house is £25,000 or less, you merely insert £25,000 so that there will be no stamp duty payable. If the price is over £25,000 but not above £30,000, insert £30,000 and the stamp duty will be ½ per cent of the price; if over £30,000 but not above £35,000, insert £35,000 and the stamp duty will be 1 per cent of the price, if over £35,000 but not above £40,000 insert £40,000 and the stamp duty will be 1½ per cent of the price. If the price is over £40,000 you insert nothing, the stamp duty is at the rate of 2 per cent of the price anyway. Matthew had inserted the figure of £40,000. He would have to pay stamp duty at the rate of 1½ per cent of the purchase price.

Lawyers tend to prepare a document in draft and submit the draft to the solicitor acting for the other person involved. So simple is the form of *Transfer of whole* that there is not much room for argument about how it should be worded; the stage of submitting the deed in draft is therefore often dispensed with.

Matthew prepared four copies of the transfer. Two of them, including the top copy, he sent to Dodds & Son. The top copy would be used as the engrossment. Therefore, he stuck a red sticker over the word 'seal' on the back page of the form, against where Mr Timms would sign. He kept one copy for his own file. The fourth copy he would shortly be sending to Hodgson, Green & Co, acting for his building society.

replies to requisitions
Dodds & Son replied to Matthew's letter of 1st February:

DODDS & SON
Solicitors   *1 Charter Street*
                                                        Minford, Surrey

                                                        4th February 1983
To: M. J. Seaton Esq

Dear Sir,

Re: 14 Twintree Avenue, Minford

We now return your Requisitions on Title, together with our replies. We
approve the form of draft transfer, and, in accordance with your suggestion, are
treating the top copy as the engrossment, and shall have this executed by our
client. We are obliged to you for the spare copies of the requisitions and of the
Transfer which you have sent for our file.

We shall be in touch with you again nearer completion date.

Yours faithfully,
Dodds & Son

Dodds & Son's answers to Matthew's requisitions on title were satisfactory.
They confirmed that their answers to the enquiries before contract still
stood, and that suitable evidence about the payment of rates and other
outgoings would be produced at completion. A completion statement
would be sent nearer the date for completion. They confirmed that the
existing mortgage in favour of the Minford Building Society would be paid
off and added that they would give an unqualified undertaking if form
53(Co) could not be handed over at completion. This meant that if the
building society holding Mr Timms' mortgage could not provide the official
form saying the mortgage was paid off, they (Dodds & Son or the building
society's solicitors) would give a personal and unqualified undertaking to
send the form on without delay. They also confirmed that vacant possession
would be given on completion and that there was no-one other than Mr
Timms in occupation of the property. Arrangements about handing over
the keys to the house would be made later. Finally they said that they would
defer until later saying where completion would take place and how and to
whom the money should be paid. With their replies, they enclosed an
additional authority to inspect the register so that Hodgson, Green & Co
could apply for an official search of the register.

the building society's solicitor

It was now time for Matthew to contact Hodgson, Green & Co, the solicitors acting for the Forthright Building Society, his proposed mortgagees.

38 Broadstone Drive
Hastings, Sussex

7th February 1983

To: Messrs Hodgson, Green & Co

Dear Sirs,

Re: 14 Twintree Avenue, Minford

Further to your letter of 21st January, I now enclose the following:
1 contract dated 27th January 1983
2 enquiries before contract and replies
3 local search certificate and enquiries with replies
4 'office copies' of the entries on the register and the filed plan
5 requisitions on title and replies
6 draft transfer as approved by the seller's solicitors
7 an authority for you to inspect the register.
   I look forward to receipt of your requisitions and the draft mortgage. The agreed completion date is 1st March; no doubt you will arrange to have the money available then.

Yours faithfully,

M. J. Seaton

He was about to part with some of the most important documents concerning his purchase and would probably never see them again because a building society keeps all the documents, as a rule. He therefore had photocopies made of the contract, the enquiries before contract and replies, the local search and enquiries with replies, office copy entries on the register and filed plan and the requisitions on titles and replies. If he had not been able to take photocopies, he would have made a note of the date when the office copy of the entries on the register was issued from the Land Registry – 5th January 1983. He would need to know this date when filling in his application for an official search of the register, nearer completion.

Matthew had a reply from Hodgson, Green & Co at the end of the week.

HODGSON, GREEN & CO
Solicitors

67 Lomax Street
Minford, Surrey

10th February 1983

To: M. J. Seaton Esq

Dear Sir,

Re: 14 Twintree Avenue, Minford

Thank you for your letter of 7th February with enclosures. We now enclose a few requisitions on title for your attention. We enclose a draft mortgage for your approval, together with a copy for your use. As you will see, the mortgage deed is in standard form and our clients do not permit variations from it.

Upon hearing from you upon these matters, we shall be sending you the engrossment mortgage deed for execution, and form of consent to be signed by your wife and any other person who will be in occupation of the house at the date of completion of the mortgage advance.

Yours faithfully,
Hodgson, Green & Co

the building society's requisitions on title

Building societies' requisitions are a list of questions about the house you are buying, covering the same sort of points as your preliminary enquiries and requisitions on title. As far as possible you should use the seller's solicitor's replies to these, to answer the building society's requisitions.

There is no one standard form in common use by building societies for these requisitions. Different solicitors use different forms; sometimes they are printed or duplicated. It may also happen that no requisitions as such are asked at all, if the title is registered; any points which need to be dealt with are then raised in a letter.

Hodgson, Green & Co had framed their own questions. The questions asked and the answers Matthew gave were as follows:

REQUISITIONS ON TITLE
SEATON – and FORTHRIGHT BUILDING SOCIETY
14 Twintree Avenue, Minford

1. Please confirm that the borrower is finding the full amount of the purchase price, apart from this mortgage loan, out of his own funds.	1. *I so confirm*
2. Please confirm that the borrower is obtaining full vacant possession of the property on completion and that no lettings of any kind are contemplated.	2. *I so confirm*
3(a). Please give the names of all persons being aged 18 or over (or approaching that age) not being parties to the mortgage deed, who will be in, or will enter into, occupation of the property at the date of completion of the mortgage.	3(a). *My wife, Emma Seaton*
3(b). Please confirm that any such person or persons will execute a form of consent postponing any interest or claim they may have in or against the property to the society's mortgage.	3(b). *Confirmed*
4. Where will completion take place?	4. *I am enquiring*
5. We shall require to receive on completion the following:	5. *Noted*

5. We shall require to receive on completion the following:
 1) Charge Certificate
 2) Form 53(Co) duly executed or an undertaking
 3) Transfer duly executed by vendor
 4) Land Registry Form A4 duly completed
 5) L(A)451 form duly completed
 6) Mortgage Deed duly executed in the presence of a solicitor
 7) Search Certificate (94A) not more than 30 days old
 8) Any requisite form of consent duly signed by any intended occupant.

With regard to 6), as you know I am not represented by a solicitor. Would it suffice if I were to execute the mortgage deed at completion, in the presence of your representative attending completion? If not what do you suggest?

Dated 10th Feb 1983.   Dated *14th Feb 1983*.

Building societies often like to know that a buyer himself is providing the whole of the rest of the money, that is, the difference between the price and the amount borrowed. They feel if the borrower has a sufficient stake of his own in the property, he is less likely to default on the mortgage. If a buyer is borrowing elsewhere, they like to be informed.

NO OTHER INTERESTED PARTIES

Question 2 firstly asked Matthew to confirm that he was obtaining full vacant possession on completion. The building society, like the buyer, has to ensure that it will not be prejudicially affected by the interests or claims of any person who was in occupation of the property with the seller before completion. The building society also likes to know that only the borrower and his family will be occupying the house; hence the reference to lettings. Understandably, the society is afraid of being landed with tenants they cannot get rid of, especially those with Rent Act protection. If the borrower defaults on his mortgage payments and the society has to sell the house, it is worth far less with tenants in it than with vacant possession. In fact, the terms of the society's offer of advance usually state that no lettings may be made. This question merely required formal confirmation.

The necessity for asking question 3 has arisen out of that House of Lords decision referred to at page 52. As well as making sure that it is not bound by the rights of anyone living in the property with the seller before completion, a building society has to be sure that it will not be bound by the rights of any person who is intending to occupy the property with the borrower. Therefore the building society requires any such person to sign a form of consent postponing (that is, not enforcing) any rights they may have in the property. Emma was the only person who was going to move into 14 Twintree Avenue with Matthew and she was quite happy to sign such a document.

PREPARING FOR COMPLETION

Question 4 asked where completion would be taking place. Matthew was not sure at the moment. The general rule is that completion takes place at the office of the seller's solicitor or of the solicitor acting for the seller's building society. Or it may be by post – but not if the buyer is without a solicitor.

Matthew knew that Mr Timms had a mortgage with the Minford Building Society which would be paid off at completion. He assumed, therefore, that completion would take place at the offices of Minford Building Society's solicitors, but as yet he did not know who they were. If Mr Timms had had no mortgage, completion would have taken place at Dodds & Son's offices.

The undertaking about form 53(Co), if one was to be provided, would come from Minford Building Society's solicitors and would provide that the form should be made available to Hodgson, Green & Co within 14 days of completion.

Finally, the list of documents which Hodgson, Green & Co would require at completion was set out at this stage to avoid any misunderstanding later.

An unusual problem presented itself at this stage: the Forthright Building Society required that the mortgage deed be executed in the presence of a solicitor, who would sign it as the witness. Although there is no requirement in law that the deed must be witnessed by a solicitor, some building societies still make this their requirement. Where a borrower is legally represented, his own solicitor is usually witness to the borrower's execution of the mortgage deed. He usually executes it some time before completion, although it does not become operative until then.

Matthew had suggested that he should execute the deed when he personally attended completion. He could then execute in the presence of the solicitor from Hodgson, Green & Co who attended completion. Alternatively, he could have taken it into any solicitor's office and executed there. All solicitors are also commissioners for oaths and will witness the execution of a document on payment of a small fee (at present, £2.50).

the mortgage deed

Hodgson, Green & Co's letter of 10th February had also enclosed the draft mortgage deed.

A famous law lord once said that 'no one . . . by the light of nature ever understood an english mortgage of real estate'. Most lawyers cannot explain the exact effect of some of the clauses in a mortgage deed without reference to a text-book, so do not be worried if you do not understand fully what it says. But if you have any queries about any particular points, ask the building society's solicitors about them.

The draft mortgage deed Matthew received was in the normal form for a building society. It was a printed document with some blank spaces in it, mainly at the beginning and the end which had been filled in with details special to his purchase.

Matthew checked that his name had been spelt correctly, that the property was correctly described and that the amount of the mortgage advance, the rate of interest and the monthly payments corresponded with the mortgage offer.

The embargo on amendments to the draft deed was quite usual. Often a building society's solicitor sends only one copy of the draft mortgage deed, so dispensing with the formality of asking the borrower or his solicitor to return one copy approved. Sometimes he sends the engrossment of the mortgage deed (with a copy) straightaway, cutting out the draft stage completely. The whole point is that you have to take it or leave it.

Matthew therefore approved the draft deed as it stood. It was a closely printed document dealing with many things, including what the society could do if he failed to make his promised payments under the mortgage. One of these was selling the property.

Even though Matthew had to admit that he did not really understand some of the other clauses, he did note some which had been referred to in the society's offer of advance of 20th January. There was one enabling the society to alter the rate of interest on giving notice, one forbidding the borrower letting the property, and one requiring the borrower to insure the property with a company to be approved by the society, 'in a sum not less than the full value thereof for the time being'.

Matthew returned the draft mortgage deed and requisitions with replies to Hodgson, Green & Co with the following letter:

> *38 Broadstone Drive*
> *Hastings, Sussex*
>
> 14th February 1983
>
> To: Messrs Hodgson, Green & Co
>
> Dear Sirs,
>
> <u>Re: 14 Twintree Avenue, Minford</u>
>
> Thank you for your letter of 10th February. I now return your requisitions with my replies, together with the draft mortgage deed approved as drawn. Thank you for the copy for my file. I look forward to hearing from you with the engrossment and the form of consent for signature by my wife Emma.
>
> I shall be grateful if you will let me know as soon as possible the amount that will be available on completion after deducting expenses.
>
> Yours faithfully,
>
> *M. J. Seaton*

It is a good idea to retain a copy of the mortgage deed in your file. The executed mortgage deed itself will be kept by the building society (or other lender) after completion.

ASKING FOR A COMPLETION STATEMENT

As well as knowing the exact amount he would be getting from the Forthright Building Society, Matthew needed to know how much money he would have to pay to Mr Timms on completion. He wrote to Dodds & Son requesting a completion statement and further details of completion.

38 Broadstone Drive
Hastings, Sussex

14th February 1983

To: Messrs Dodds & Son

Dear Sirs,

Re: 14 Twintree Avenue, Minford

I refer to your letter of 4th February, and shall be obliged if you will let me have a completion statement made up to 1st March, as soon as possible.
Presumably you will require the sum to be paid in the form of a banker's draft?
    Please arrange for the keys to be handed over at completion, or if more convenient to be left with the agents.
    Can you now let me know where completion will take place?

Yours faithfully,

M. J. Seaton

It is the usual practice between solicitors to carry out the financial side of the transfer of property by banker's draft. This is recognised by both sets of conditions of sale. The Law Society's condition 21(2) provides that the draft must be drawn by and upon a member of the Committee of the London Clearing Bankers, a trustee savings bank or National Girobank. The members of the Committee of London Clearing Bankers are: Barclays Bank, Coutts, Lloyds Bank, Midland Bank, National Westminster Bank and Williams & Glyn's Bank.

In the National Conditions, condition 5(3) says that the banker's draft must be issued by a 'designated bank'. The list of designated banks includes most commercial banks.

TELEGRAPHIC TRANSFERS

Sometimes it is necesary or desirable to have a sale and a purchase completed at the same time, so that the purchase money received on the sale can be applied towards the purchase, and the buyer can move out of his old and into his new home on the same day.

This operation is relatively simple if the parties are within easy reach of each other. The sale can be completed in the morning and the draft for the purchase money endorsed over to the seller's solicitors in an afternoon completion.

But where the parties are too distant from each other for this procedure to be carried out, a buyer's solicitor can complete the purchase by 'credit or telegraphic transfer'.

The procedure is as follows: the buyer's solicitor obtains details of the seller's solicitor's bank and the number of the account into which he pays clients' money (called a client account) and arranges for the completion money to be paid direct to that account by credit transfer from his bank to the other. The seller's solicitor's bank is asked to telephone its customer the minute the credit is received; the seller's solicitor then telephones the selling agents advising them that completion has taken place and asking them to release the keys to the buyer. The completion documents are then sent through the post.

It is not recommended that a buyer attempt this method of completing without a solicitor (even if he has the necessary money and does not have to rely on a solicitor's undertaking to obtain bridging finance), because of the risk of something not being quite right if he cannot check the documents himself.

building society's solicitors
Matthew had a reply from Hodgson, Green & Co first:

HODGSON, GREEN & CO
Solicitors   *67 Lomax Street*
                                                                                Minford, Surrey

                                                                          17th February 1983
To: M. J. Seaton Esq

Dear Sir,

Re: 14 Twintree Avenue, Minford

We thank you for your letter of 14th February. With regard to your query on our requisition 5(6), it will be quite in order if you execute the mortgage deed (the engrossment of which we now enclose) at completion in the presence of the writer, assuming of course that completion takes place in this town. If it does not, it would be necessary for you to make an alternative arrangement about executing the mortgage.

We enclose a copy of the society's rules for your retention.

We further enclose a statement showing £31,071.70 as being available on completion, after deducting the expenses shown. If it is required that this sum be provided in split drafts, please let us know as soon as possible, and in any event not later than 3 days before completion, the amount of each draft and to whom it should be payable.

We finally enclose the Form of Consent for signature by your wife, Mrs Emma Seaton. The form should be signed in the presence of a witness.

Yours faithfully,
Hodgson, Green & Co

Matthew checked that the engrossment of the mortgage deed was in accordance with the draft which he had approved. He left it unsigned and undated. This would be done at completion.

Hodgson, Green & Co enclosed a copy of the rules of the Forthright Building Society for Matthew to keep. He had, in fact, got a copy of these already as he had been saving with the society for some years, and was an established member. If he is not one already, a potential borrower must become a member of the society that will lend him money, but such membership is little more than a formality.

WHAT WILL BE DEDUCTED

Rather more important for the moment was the statement which Hodgson, Green & Co sent with their letter, showing how much of the loan would be left after the expenses had been deducted.

SEATON AND FORTHRIGHT BUILDING SOCIETY
re: 14 Twintree Avenue, Minford, Surrey

	£		£
Mortgage advance			32,000.00
Deductions:			
1) stamp duty on transfer at £40,000	600.00		
2) Land Registry fees	98.00		
3) our costs (inc VAT)	140.30		
4) insurance premium	90.00		
		less	928,30
Net sum available at completion			31,071.70

These expenses were Matthew's main expenses of the whole transaction. They were deducted from his mortgage advance because after completion Hodgson, Green & Co would take away the transfer, mortgage deed and other documents which were their client society's security for the loan. They would attend to the stamping of the transfer, and the registration of it and of the mortgage at the Land Registry. Where title to property is registered, the buyer has to register the transfer of ownership to him and is charged a fee for doing this. Land Registry fees are on a scale, and the amounts depend on the purchase price. The mortgage is also registered, but no fee is charged for doing this if it is done at the same time as registering the change of proprietorship. The stamp duty and land registry fees would be paid by Hodgson, Green & Co, but were Matthew's responsibility; hence the deduction.

Hodgson, Green & Co's legal costs fell into much the same category. They naturally wished to be sure that they would be paid, and Matthew had been told in the offer of advance that he would have to bear their costs. A scale of fees to be paid to a solicitor who deals with the legal side of a building society mortgage applies if the solicitor is also acting for the purchaser. Where a solicitor is acting for the building society only, he may charge whatever is a 'fair and reasonable' fee (this is not likely to be more than 60 per cent more than the 'acting-for-both' scale fee) or the Building Societies Association's 'recommended' fee.

Finally, the insurance premium was deducted. The house had been insured with the Bridstow Insurance Company since exchange of contracts. To make sure that the property was insured, the society had paid the first premium and deducted it from their loan. The insurance had been based on the reinstatement value of the house, that is the cost of rebuilding it should it be totally destroyed, not its present value. Thus 14 Twintree Avenue was insured for £60,000 not £40,000. The Bridstow Insurance Company charged an annual premium at the rate of £1.50 for every £1000 of the amount insured for their comprehensive insurance on a house. On £60,000 this was £90.00.

Matthew checked the figures for each of these deductions; each one was correct.

The final enclosure with Hodgson, Green & Co's letter was the form of consent which Emma had to sign:

FORM OF CONSENT

Property Address: *14 Twintree Avenue, Minford, Surrey*
Name of Borrower: *Matthew John Seaton*

WHEREAS FORTHRIGHT BUILDING SOCIETY ('the society') proposes to make an advance to the borrower upon the security of a mortgage or charge over the proprty in the society's current form.

NOW I the undernamed being a person who will be in occupation of the property HEREBY CONSENT to the creation of such mortgage or charge over the property to secure such advance and UNDERTAKE to the society that such rights and interest if any as I may have in or over the property shall be postponed and made subject to the rights and interest of the society under the mortgage or charge.

Signed by (occupant)............................. on (date).....................
In the presence of (witness)...

The form had a note on the bottom advising the occupant to consult a solicitor if he or she was not clear of the legal implications in executing the form. Emma recognised the legal implications involved and was willing to execute the form. She would sign it in front of her neighbour, as witness, that weekend. The witness does not have to be a solicitor or anyone in authority. But Matthew could not witness her signature, because he was the proposed borrower, lest it should appear that Emma had been coerced by him to sign the consent.

completion statement

On monday, Matthew had a letter from Dodds & Son:

DODDS & SON
Solicitors

1 Charter Street
Minford, Surrey

18th February 1983

To: M. J. Seaton Esq

Dear Sir,

Re: 14 Twintree Avenue, Minford

We now enclose completion statement made up to 1st March. Completion will take place at the offices of Messrs Anderson, James & Pringle, 88 Great Winchester Street, Minford, solicitors for the existing mortgagees. We confirm that the balance required to complete must be paid by banker's draft and split as indicated in the note on the completion statement. We have noted what you say about the keys.

Yours faithfully,
Dodds & Son

The completion statement read as follows:

TIMMS TO SEATON
14 TWINTREE AVENUE, MINFORD, SURREY
COMPLETION STATEMENT
made up to 1st March 1983

	£	£
Purchase price		40,000.00
Less deposit		4,000.00
		36,000.00

Add:

	£	£
Proportion of general rates from 1st March to 31st March 1983 (31 days) at £472 per annum	40.09	
Proportion of water rates for same period (31 days) at £49 per annum	4.16	
Proportion of water services charge for same period (31 days) at £51 per annum	4.33	
		48.58
Balance payable on completion		36,048.58

NB 1. Please produce deposit release at completion
   2. Please provide above sum in two drafts in favour of:
   (i) Minford Building Society for   £ 3,738.08
   (ii) Ourselves (Dodds & Son) for £32,310.50
   £36,048.58

APPORTIONMENTS

About a week to ten days before completion the seller's solicitor sends the buyer or his solicitor a completion statment showing the exact amount that he will require on completion: purchase price, less deposit, plus or minus an apportionment of general and water rate and water services charge (sewerage facilities) depending on whether at the date of completion it is in arrears or has been paid in advance. The seller is responsible for outgoings up to and including the day before completion, while the buyer is responsible from and including the actual completion day. In Matthew's case, the general and water rate and water services charges had been paid up until 1st April 1983, so Matthew had to pay the part of these, namely 31 days, attributable to the period 1st March to 31st March.

It is, in fact, not necessary for the outgoings to be apportioned. The seller's solicitor can write to the rating and water authorities informing them of the sale and the completion date, with the full name of the buyer and asking for an apportioned figure for the seller up to completion. If the outgoings have been paid in advance, the seller will get a refund; if not, it is common practice for him to give an undertaking to the buyer (handed over at completion) to pay these up to completion. It is unnecessary for the buyer to give an undertaking to pay them from completion, because he has to pay them anyway.

In the case of leasehold property, the ground rent payable to the landlord and the annual insurance premium have also to be apportioned. Ground rent is usually paid to the landlord in arrears on each quarter day, or half-yearly. As a rule, the insurance premium has to be apportioned because the buyer has no option but to take over the existing policy if the lease so requires. The apportionment of the insurance premium is made from exchange of contract, when the property started to be at the buyer's risk.

To apportion liability for gas and electricity, the seller arranges to have the meters read on the day he gives possession to the buyer. Separate bills are then sent to each. If the telephone is being taken over, the rental should be apportioned.

Where, like Matthew, you have paid a small deposit as 'earnest' money to an agent who holds it as stakeholder, you will be asked to hand over a deposit release on completion. This can be in the simple form of a letter addressed to the agent asking him to release the deposit to the seller.

The completion statement will also tell you how the seller's solicitor wants the purchase money to be paid; whether he wants it all by way of banker's drafts in his favour or whether he wants some of it in favour of another firm, for example, the seller's building society's solicitor. This is where matters can become complicated for a buyer, because you have to bring the right amount of money with you to completion. The difficulty does not derive from the law but from the diversity of most buyers' financial resources. For example, you may be buying a house with the aid of a building society mortgage and provide the balance from the sale of your present house, out of the proceeds of which you have to pay off an existing mortgage; your seller's solicitor has asked for two drafts: one in his favour, and one in favour of the seller's building society.

It is really just a question of sitting down and working out where the money is coming from and going to. It may help to remember that if part of your purchase price is coming from the proceeds of a simultaneous sale of your own house, then, provided that the banker's draft you get on your sale is in your favour and not crossed 'account payee only', you can use it for your purchase (by endorsing it) without having to put it through your bank. Alternatively, you can ask your buyer's solicitor to split the money for your house into two separate banker's drafts if required by your seller's solicitor, or possibly into three if you have an existing mortgage to pay off.

Matthew's financial calculations were going to be relatively simple because he had only been asked for two drafts: one in favour of the Minford Building Society which would be used to discharge Mr Timms' existing mortgage, and the other (for the balance) in favour of Dodds & Son.

PRACTICAL MATTERS

It was a very busy time for Matthew and the legal side of the purchase was not the only matter that was taking up his time. There was also the sorting and packing and clearing out the rented house they were living in, arranging for removal men, for having the meters read, getting change of address cards prepared and sent off and all the other rigmarole of getting ready for moving.

He learnt on the telephone from Mr Timms that he had arranged to move out of 14 Twintree Avenue on 28th February, so that the house would be ready for the Seatons on 1st March. Unless a special arrangement is made, the seller does not let a buyer take possession until completion has actually taken place and the money handed over. There might be a last minute hitch which could conceivably result in the sale never being completed, in which case things might be very awkward for the seller if the buyer had already moved in.

It is however very important for the buyer to make sure that the house has been totally vacated before handing over the purchase money, and that there is no-one in the house.

It is a good idea to arrange (if you can) to have the keys before completion, so that you can inspect the house on completion day. Mr Timms would not agree to give Matthew the keys early but he did promise to arrange for Flint & Morgan to let Matthew into the house on the morning of the 1st of March.

Matthew wrote to Dodds & Son:

38 Broadstone Drive
Hastings, Sussex

21st February 1983

To: Messrs Dodds & Son

Dear Sirs,

<u>Re: 14 Twintree Avenue, Minford</u>

Thank you for your letter of 18th February enclosing the completion statement. I note that the amount required to complete is £36,048.58 of which £3,738.08 is to go to the Minford Building Society.

I understand that your client is moving out on 28th February and that the keys will be handed over by you at completion. Is this right?

I shall be moving in during the afternoon of 1st March, all being well. An appointment for completion at, say, 12 noon would suit me. Would you let me know whether this is acceptable to Messrs Anderson, James & Pringle? The solicitors for my mortgagees, Messrs Hodgson, Green & Co, are able to fit in with this suggestion.

Yours faithfully,

M. J. Seaton

Completion usually takes place before 2.30pm on the day in question, for banking purposes. Unless the special conditions of sale in the contract provide otherwise, the Law Society's conditions state that completion shall take place by 2.30pm, otherwise it counts as a day later. The National conditions mention completion time only for a friday: if it does not take place by 2.15pm, it is deemed to take place on the following monday.

Matthew had already telephoned Hodgson, Green & Co informing them of the venue for completion. 12 noon had been a suitable time for them, and he subsequently heard that it was also convenient for Dodds & Son and Anderson, James & Pringle.

Matthew wrote to Hodgson, Green & Co mainly to confirm what he had already told them on the telephone:

38 Broadstone Drive
Hastings, Sussex

21st February 1983

To: Messrs Hodgson, Green & Co

Dear Sirs,

14 Twintree Avenue, Minford

I received your letter of 17th February and note what you say regarding execution of the mortgage deed and form of consent.

I have now received a completion statement from the seller's solicitors and can tell you how the amount to be made available at completion should be split. Please provide the sum of £31,071.70 in two drafts as follows:

1) in favour of Minford Building Society   £ 3,738.08
2) in favour of Dodds & Son   £27,333.62
                                                             £31,071.70

I confirm our telephone conversation to the effect that completion is to take place at the offices of Messrs Anderson, James & Pringle of 88 Great Winchester Street, Minford on 1st March. The suggested time for completion is 12 noon. I will let you know when and if this time is confirmed.

Yours faithfully,

M. J. Seaton

This meant that Matthew would only have to request one draft from his bank: for £4,976.88 in favour of Dodds & Son, to make up the balance of the amount due on completion of £36,048.58.

He subsequently telephoned Hodgson, Green & Co to confirm that completion would take place at 12 noon.

NOTES IN PREPARATION FOR COMPLETION

Matthew prepared for his own use a memorandum for completion:

14 Twintree Avenue: completion 12 noon on 1st March 1983 at Anderson, James & Pringle, 88 Great Winchester Street, Minford.

Price and costs		£
Price of house		40,000.00
Stamp duty on transfer		600.00
Land registry fees		98.00
Hodgson, Green & Co's fees		140.30
Insurance premium		90.00
Building society valuation fee		58.65
Own survey fee		150.00
Local search fees		12.90
Proportion of rates, water charges etc		48.58
Total		41,198.43
offer of advance	less	32,000.00
		9,198.43
What I actually pay or paid		
Deposit (10 per cent)		4,000.00
Building society's valuation fee		58.65
Own survey fee		150.00
Local search fees		12.90
Dodds & Son, at completion		4,976.88
		9,198.43

I must take with me: search certificate (form 94A),
Land Registry application (form A4),
Stamps L(A) 451 form,
mortgage deed,
form of consent,
banker's draft payable to Dodds & Son for £4,976.88.

Hodgson, Green & Co (acting for Forthright Building Society) will require from me: Search certificate (form 94A), Land Registry application (form A4), Stamps L(A) 451 form, mortgage deed, form of consent.

Hodgson, Green & Co will require from Anderson, James & Pringle (acting for Minford Building Society): charge certificate, form 53(Co) or an undertaking to discharge the existing mortgage.

Hodgson, Green & Co will require from Dodds & Son (acting for Mr Timms): transfer executed by Mr Timms.

Dodds & Son (acting for Mr Timms) will require from me: banker's draft for £4,976.88; they will require from Hodgson, Green & Co bankers draft for £27,333.62.

Anderson, James & Pringle (acting for Minford Building Society) will require from Hodgson, Green & Co: banker's draft for £3,738.08.

I will require from Dodds & Son: keys, receipts for general rate, water rate and water services charge.

Money (ie banker's drafts)	£	£
from me		4,976.88
from Forthright BS	3,738.08	
from Forthright BS	27,333.62	
		31,071.70
due per completion statement		36,048.58
split thus:		
to Minford BS (from Forthright BS)		3,738.07
to Dodds & Son from (Forthright BS)	27,333.62	
from me	4,976.88	
		32,310.50
		36,048.58

The memorandum set out the essence of what would happen on completion. It served a double function: a reminder to Matthew, and a summary of the financial side of the purchase.

official search

Tuesday 22nd February was ringed in red in Matthew's diary; he had to send off his application for an official search of the register at the Land Registry.

This search is done on form 94A if you are buying the whole of the land comprised in the title; form 94B if you are buying part only (say one house out of ten). An application on form 94B must usually be accompanied by a plan. Both forms are simple to fill in if you follow their wording and instructions carefully.

Matthew used form 94A. At the top of the form was a box for the name of the district land registry to which the form was being sent. There is a list of district land registries (with telephone numbers) on the back of the form. If you do not know which district land registry covers the district in which you are buying your house, telephone any one of these for the information. Surrey is covered by Tunbridge Wells registry, so Matthew sent his form there.

Underneath was a large square panel divided into six sections. The first three required details of the county and district, title number of the property and full name of the registered proprietor. Matthew took these off the copy of the office copy entries which he had made earlier. The fourth section read 'Application is made to ascertain whether any adverse entry has been made in the register since the date shown opposite being either the date on which an office copy of the subsisting entries in the register was issued or the last date on which the land or charge certificate was officially examined with the register.' The date required here is that shown on the bottom of the office copy entries; in Matthew's case, 5th January 1983. In the unlikely event of your having been supplied with an ordinary copy (not an office copy) of the seller's title, it will have a date written on it by the seller's solicitor, namely on the inside cover of the actual land or charge certificate. This is the date on which the land or charge certificate was examined and brought up to date by the Land Registry and is the date that should be inserted on the form.

In the fifth section Matthew wrote his full name; he was the applicant for the search. The sixth section only applies where a solicitor is making the search on the buyer's behalf.

Underneath this Matthew had to put an X in box B (which applied where the applicant was not a solicitor). The cross indicated that the written authority of the registered proprietor, Mr Timms, to inspect the register accompanied the form. Without such authority the buyer cannot make his search. At the bottom of the form was a space to fill in the name and address to which the form should be sent. Matthew filled in his own.

The form has a tear-off duplicate which must also be filled in, the original being returned to the applicant with the certificate on the back date-stamped by the Land Registry.

The search form is a device to warn you off and protect you from any adverse entries put on the register since the date of the office copy entries or when the land certificate was last compared with the register. It is essential for the buyer to have obtained the search certificate back from the Land Registry before completion actually takes place. He should never complete without it.

When the Land Registry sends back an official search certificate, it confirms that no adverse entry has been made since the date searched from. If it says something other than this, do not complete. A building society will not release its loan without a search certificate.

PRIORITY
The search certificate says another thing, namely that if the buyer applies

to be registered as owner before 11am on the thirtieth working day from the date of the certificate, no-one else can be registered as owner in the meantime. This is what is meant by saying that a search gives a priority period of thirty working days.

So, the time factor is important in the case of an official search of the register.

The search form should be sent off about 5 working days before completion; ideally the certificate should be dated the day before completion. The point of this is to ensure that the buyer gets the full benefit of the period of priority which his certificate of search gives him.

Sending off the search form as near to completion as possible allows time to attend to the stamping of the transfer and other formalities before lodging the application to register the transfer.

The Land Registry is usually reliable about searches, and district land registries send their replies by first class mail, often by return of post, to all searches received by first post. You can telephone the district land registry concerned to find out what is the current delay in dealing with searches. In an emergency, a search can be made by telephone; details of making a search by telephone can be found in the land registry pamphlet *Official searches of the register* available on request from any district land registry.

If there is any delay in completing your purchase, you should make a second search.

Matthew posted form 94A together with his authority to inspect the register (which Dodds & Son had sent him with their letter of 27th January) by first class post to Tunbridge Wells District Land Registry. No fee is payable for the search.

land charges search

Another official search which a buyer may be asked to make is a search in the Land Charges Registry. This is in Plymouth and is quite distinct from the Land Registry at Lincoln's Inn Fields, London and the district land registries.

The Land Charges Register is really only meant for cases where the title to property is unregistered but sometimes a building society asks for a search to be made in it by the buyer, even though the property has a registered title. This is because such a search will reveal whether the buyer has been made bankrupt, something the search on form 94A will not reveal. This is of obvious interest to a building society lending thousands of pounds. A Land Charges search gives 15 working days' priority.

The form on which application is made to the Land Charges Registry is form K16; the only information sought is whether or not the buyer is bankrupt. The name and address of the buyer must be filled in; there are columns in the form for this. A Land Registry stamp (from head post offices) for 50p for each name searched should be stuck on the form in the space at the top. The result (certificate) of the search will be returned by the Land Charges Registry within a week.

If you are pressed for time, perhaps because your building society has sprung a requisition for a clear bankruptcy form on you a week before completion, it may help to ring the Land Charges Registry at Plymouth 779831 before sending off your form K16, and ask to whom you should address your request in order to get the search certificate quickly. It is also possible to get a telephone search (with confirmation of the results within 24 hours) but only for someone (such as Oyez and most solicitors) who has credit facilities with the Land Charges Registry. Some building societies' solicitors mention the bankruptcy clearance as part of their normal requisition; some do not bother with it. Matthew had not been asked to supply this Land Charges search.

While he was filling in forms he thought he might as well fill in the other two, form A4 and the LA form that would have to be ready to be handed over to Hodgson, Green & Co at completion.

preparing form A4

A buyer becomes the full legal owner of registered property only when he is registered as the new proprietor at the Land Registry, not when the property is actually transferred to him on completion. The Land Registration Act lays down no time-limit within which a buyer must apply to be registered as the new proprietor, but to take advantage of the priority period conferred by his official search certificate, a buyer should lodge his application for registration before the thirty day period expires. Since an average interval of about three months elapses between the date of application for registration and the actual date of registration, and the buyer must be protected from any intermediate dealings with the property by the seller, registration is deemed to take place on the date the application is delivered to the Land Registry.

The buyer applies to the Land Registry to have his name entered as the registered proprietor on form A4 – *Application to register dealings with the whole of the land comprised in registered title*. If buying part of land with registered title, use form A5, which is in similar terms. Form A4 is simple to fill in. It consists of four pages, the inside two being for Land Registry use only.

At the top of the front page of form A4 is a space for the County and District (or London borough) in which the property is situated and the title number. Then follows a space to state the 'nature and priority of applications'. Matthew was in fact making three applications; first the removal, or discharge of Mr Timms' mortgage; secondly, Matthew's name would have to be substituted for Mr Timms as the name of the registered proprietor; thirdly, details of Matthew's mortgage to the Forthright Building Society would have to be entered in the charges register. He therefore filled in this part of the form as follows:

Nature and priority of applications	Value	Fee scale para or abatement	£ p
Discharge of mortgage	—	—	—
Transfer	£40,000.00	4	98.00
Mortgage	£32,000.00	abatement	
		Total fees paid	98.00

There is no Land Registry fee payable on the discharge of a mortgage. The Land Registry fee for a transfer is charged according to 'Land Registry fee scale 4' calculated on the price of the house. The value of the buyer's mortgage must be stated, but where a mortgage and transfer are registered simultaneously, the normal Land Registry fee for a mortage is reduced (abated to nil). 'Abatement' should be inserted in column three.

The next part of the form is headed 'Panel 1 – Documents lodged herewith'. Matthew listed six: charge certificate, form 53(Co), transfer, search certificate on form 94A, mortgage and copy of the mortgage. The Land Registry require a copy of the mortgage to be lodged with the application. Hodgson, Green & Co would provide a copy for this purpose. (The copy counts as a separate document.)

Panel 1 also asked for the 'Name and address of solicitor or applicant to whom the acknowledgement of the application and all requisitions made by the Land Registry including requests for unpaid fees are to be sent'. Where the buyer buys with the help of a mortgage, the application is sent or lodged with the Land Registry by the lender or the lender's solicitor. Matthew wrote there the name and address of Hodgson, Green & Co.

If you are buying without the aid of a mortgage, insert your own name and address.

Sometimes a document lodged with an application to the Land Registry has to be returned to someone other than the applicant after the Land Registry has dealt with the application, for instance, if it deals with other property as well as that to which the application relates. This is unlikely to be the case with property within the scope of this book; panel 2 should be left blank.

Panel 3 on the back of the form asks for the full postal addresses of the new proprietor of the land and the new proprietor of the charge. Matthew inserted his own and the Forthright Building Society's addresses respectively there. Since he would be moving into 14 Twintree Avenue immediately after completion, that was the address he used.

Panel 4 deals with joint ownership. It asks you to state whether or not the survivor can give a valid receipt for the proceeds of sale of the property. You should insert here 'yes' if you have agreed to hold the property as joint tenants or 'no' if you have agreed to hold it as tenants in common. Panel 4 did not apply in Matthew's case.

Panel 5 deals with where a limited company is buying property or lending money on mortgage. Panel 6 applies where a mortgage is finally paid off. Neither were applicable here.

At the bottom of the form is a space to fill in the amount of the land registry fee and sign the form. Hodgson, Green & Co would sign the form and send it off to the Land Registry with their cheque for the fees, after completion and after they had attended to the stamping of the transfer.

It is important to deliver the application before the priority period conferred by the official search certificate expires. Building society solicitors can be notoriously slow in sending form A4 and the documents to the Land Registry for registration, so ask your building society solicitor, at completion, not to delay in sending off the application even if this means not waiting for form 53(Co) to arrive. That can be forwarded later.

A buyer without a mortgage has to attend to these matters himself. After completion, you should get your transfer stamped and send form A4 and the documents (land certificate or charge certificate and form 53(Co), transfer and search certificate on form 94A) to the Land Registry to arrive within your priority period.

preparing form Stamps L(A) 451

Any instrument (deed) transferring freehold or leasehold land has to be produced to the Inland Revenue, together with a statement of particulars about the instrument, within 30 days of its execution (completion). If stamp duty is payable, the transfer is stamped with the duty paid. Even if no stamp duty is payable (because the price is under £25,000) the instrument still has to be produced and is stamped showing that its particulars have been delivered. A fine of up to £50 is payable for non-compliance. The Land Registry will not register a new owner unless the transfer to him has been duly stamped.

The simplest and now universal method of supplying the particulars required by the Inland Revenue is to use form Stamps L(A) 451, commonly known as a PD form or LA form. The form is available from Inland Revenue stamp offices, from some head post offices, or by post from the Controller of Stamps Office, South West Wing, Bush House, Strand, London WC2B 4QN. If you have any difficulty in obtaining the form, walk into any solicitors' office and ask them nicely for one or, if your courage fails you, ask your building society's (or other lender's) solicitor to send you one.

The form is headed *Particulars of Instruments Transferring or Leasing Land*, and is divided into panels. In panel 1, Description of Instrument write: transfer. The date of the instrument (panel 2) should be left blank until completion. Panels 3 and 4 call for the names and addresses of the transferor or lessor and transferee or lessee. In here should be written the names and addresses of the seller and the buyer; in Matthew's case, Mr Timms and himself.

In panel 5 the 'situation of the land' must be stated. Matthew simply wrote '14 Twintree Avenue, Minford, Surrey'. The rating authority is also asked for; in his case Minford D.C. Panel 6 requires details of the 'estate or interest transferred'. Matthew wrote 'freehold'. Had he been buying a leasehold house he would have stated 'Remainder of ..... years lease from (date), at the rent of £..... per annum.'

Panel 7 asks for the 'Consideration' and gives a list ((a)–(f)) of alternative forms of payment; (a) will apply to most buyers, who will pay money for their house. Against capital payment in 7(a) Matthew wrote '£40,000'. Panels 8 and 9 will not normally be applicable; they relate to the creation of new mineral or sporting rights, restrictive convenants and so on. Matthew put 'nil' in both panels. Hodgson, Green & Co would be attending to stamping the transfer on his behalf after completion. He wrote their name and address in panel 12, asking for the 'name and address of signatory if other than transferee or lessee'. Panel 11 requires details of the transferor's or lessor's solicitor. In here he put the name and address of Dodds & Son, Mr Timms' solicitors.

before completion

On friday 25th February, Matthew's official search certificate on form 94A arrived back from the Land Registry with its reassuring message: 'Since the 5th day of January 1983 NO ADVERSE ENTRY HAS BEEN MADE THEREON'. This meant that there had been no change in the register since the office copy entries that Dodds & Son had sent him, were issued. The certificate was dated 24th February 1983 and under this date it said 'Priority expires 11th April 1983'. This was the thirtieth working day (allowing for Easter) after the date of the issue of the certificate.

It may reassure the buyer to know that most solicitors in many years of practice will have never had a Land Registry search form returned with any adverse entry noted on it; the chances are very rare. If you are one of the unlucky ones and your search form is returned with particulars of an entry on the register since the date of your office copy entries and such an entry is a second charge (that is, mortgage) it can be dealt with in the same way as if it had happened on the office copies. If the charge is to a building society, it must be included in the undertaking that it will be redeemed before completion. Or you should insist that form 53 (which applies where the lender is an individual) or form 53(Co) (the lender is a company or building society) be handed over at completion. If the entry relates to anything else, do not go ahead with the transaction without consulting a solicitor.

Also on 25th February, Matthew telephoned his bank manager and (having made the necessary arrangements previously) ordered a banker's draft for £4,976.88 payable to Dodds & Son. He wrote out the release of deposit that he would have to hand over at completion.

38 Broadstone Drive
Hastings, Sussex

1st March 1983

To: Messrs Flint & Morgan

Dear Sirs,

Re: 14 Twintree Avenue, Minford

Completion of my purchase of this property having today taken place, I authorise and request you to account for the deposit of £100 in your hands to Messrs Dodds & Son, the seller's solicitors, or as they direct.

Yours faithfully,

M. J. Seaton

YOU MUST GET VACANT POSSESSION

He also telephoned Flint & Morgan to check that Mr Timms had made the necessary arrangements with them for him to inspect the property on the morning of completion. The importance of a buyer doing this (or having someone do it on his behalf) cannot be overstressed. Vacant possession must be given on completion. Getting rid of squatters can be a lengthy process. If you find someone living there who refuses to go, do not complete.

If a buyer cannot get vacant possession, he should immediately notify the seller's solicitor: it is, in the first place, the seller's problem because he has contracted to give vacant possession on completion. The buyer should also, as a matter of courtesy, inform his bank and building society's solicitor of what is happening. And he will have to obtain the help of a solicitor if vacant possession is not given within a reasonable time, say, two weeks.

completion day

Tuesday 1st March 1983 was hectic for the Seatons and was made more so by Matthew having to detach himself from the general operation and attend to his completion. He collected together the documents he would need: the certificate of search (form 94A), Land Registry application (form A4), form Stamps L(A) 451, the mortgage deed and the form of consent signed by Emma, and the release of deposit letter.

He went first to his bank in Hastings to collect the banker's draft in favour of Dodds & Son for £4,976.88 and then straight on to Minford. He met Mr Morgan, the estate agent outside 14 Twintree Avenue, and together they inspected the house thoroughly. No, there were no signs of anyone living there. The time was fast approaching 12 noon so he bade farewell to Mr Morgan and proceeded to 88 Great Winchester Street.

Pausing for one moment outside the rambling victorian offices of Messrs Anderson, James & Pringle he recalled the words from Dickens' *Bleak House*, 'in those shrunken fragments of its greatness, lawyers lie like maggots in nuts'. Inside, he was shown into an office where the solicitors of Anderson, James & Pringle, Dodds & Son and Hodgson, Green & Co awaited him, ready to get down to business.

THE CHARGE CERTIFICATE

After the usual introductions, Anderson, James & Pringle produced the charge certificate, which was handed to Matthew via Dodds & Son. He checked to see that it was the same as the office copy entries he was sent at the outset. If you were sent a photocopy of the land or charge certificate, as distinct from an office copy, you should also see that the date stamped on the inside cover of the land or charge certificate is the same date as you were given, and quoted on your search form. Matthew passed the charge certificate to Hodgson, Green & Co, who also examined it. With the charge certificate were a bundle of old documents – local search certificates, enquiries and requisitions, collected from when the property had changed hands before.

FORM 53(Co) OR AN UNDERTAKING

Next, Anderson, James & Pringle produced an undertaking regarding form 53(Co) which, on request, they addressed to Hodgson, Green & Co.
It read as follows:

ANDERSON, JAMES & PRINGLE
Solicitors   *88 Great Winchester Street*
                                                          Minford, Surrey

                                                          1st March 1983

To: Messrs Hodgson, Green & Co

Dear Sirs,

Re: 14 Twintree Avenue, Minford

As solicitors for the Minford Building Society, we hereby undertake to forward you form 53(Co) duly executed by the society within fourteen days.

Yours faithfully,
Anderson, James & Pringle

Another way of dealing with this matter is for the seller's solicitors to provide the undertaking, on the basis that it is the seller's responsibility to see that his mortgage is properly paid off and evidence of the paying off given to the purchaser. The form of such an undertaking would be like this:

'In consideration of your today completing the purchase of 14 Twintree
Avenue, Minford, we hereby undertake forthwith to pay over to the Minford
Building Society the money required to redeem the mortgage dated 1st
November 1971 and to forward form 53(Co) to you as soon as it is received by
us from the Minford Building Society.

Dodds & Son'

THE TRANSFER

Dodds & Son then handed Matthew the transfer. He checked that this was
the same document he had filled in and that it had been signed by Mr Timms
in the presence of a witness. Although not strictly necessary, the witness
should countersign and add his address. It was agreed that Dodds & Son
should date the transfer '1st March 1983'. Matthew transcribed these
details onto his copy of the transfer, so that he had a complete copy. This
done, he handed the transfer to Hodgson, Green & Co.

THE MORTGAGE DEED

Matthew now produced and signed the mortgage deed in the presence of
the solicitor from Hodgson, Green & Co, who countersigned as witness.
The deed was again dated '1st March 1983'. The date when the first
monthly payment was to be made was also inserted into the deed. Matthew
put these details into his copy of the mortgage deed so that he had a
complete copy of that document too. The actual deed was then taken by
Hodgson, Green & Co.

Matthew handed to Hodgson, Green & Co his Land Registry application
form (form A4), the form Stamps L(A) 451 and the consent signed by
Emma. Finally, he gave them his official search certificate (form 94A)
showing a clear search.

Dodds & Son produced receipts for the current half-year's rates, water
rates and water services charge. Matthew compared the figures shown on
them with those on the completion statement and handed the receipts
back. Finally they handed Matthew the keys to 14 Twintree Avenue.

THE MONEY

Now for the money! Matthew handed his banker's draft for £4,976.88 to
Dodds & Son. Hodgson, Green & Co then handed two banker's drafts to
Matthew. This was the correct procedure, as they (on behalf of the
Forthright Building Society) were doing business only with Matthew and

with no one else present. Matthew examined the drafts and saw that they had been made out as requested; one for £3,738.08 payable to Minford Building Society and the other for £27,333.62 payable to Dodds & Son. He handed both to Dodds & Son: he had no direct relationship with the Minford Building Society. Dodds & Son checked both drafts and handed the one for £3,738.08 to Anderson, James & Pringle.

Completion was over.

completion by post

When the parties are a considerable distance from each other, a simple conveyancing transaction can, by arrangement, be completed through the post. In such a case the buyer, or his solicitor, sends the seller's solicitors a banker's draft, crossed for safety in the post, in favour of those solicitors on their undertaking that on its receipt they will send by return of post the transfer, land certificate and all other relevant documents to the buyer or his solicitor.

delay in completion

Time is not of the essence as far as the completion date is concerned, unless the special conditions of sale in the contract provide otherwise. In other words, it is not an essential term of the contract that the parties complete on the specified date. However, especially in chain transactions, the possible consequences of delay can be quite harsh: both sets of conditions of sale (National condition of sale 5(2); Law Society's general condition of sale 22) provide that either party has the right to recover damages for the other's delay in completing. It is therefore important for both the seller and the buyer to make every effort possible to complete on time.

If there is delay and it continues, either party can serve a 'special notice to complete'. Once served, time becomes of the essence. Under condition 22 of the National Conditions, the party in default then has 16 working days to complete the contract; under 23(4) of the Law Society's general conditions, twenty-one working days. If the buyer fails to comply with the notice, the seller can forfeit the deposit and claim damages for any loss he suffers on re-sale. If the seller fails to comply, the buyer can recover his deposit and claim damages for any loss suffered.

after completion

Matthew had no more legal formalities to attend to after completion, but this would not have been the case, had he been buying a leasehold house.

The buyer must usually notify the landlord's solicitor that the lease has been transferred to him.

Some leases demand that the transfer itself should be produced to the landlord's solicitor for inspection and return. Even if it does, the buyer need only send a copy. If the lease requires no more than that the landlord should be notified of the change of ownership, the buyer merely has to write a letter to the landlord's solicitor saying 'The property known as ...... comprised in the lease dated ...... for a term of ..... years was transferred on ..... to ...... of ......'. It is usual to send the notification in duplicate, getting the landlord's solicitor to sign an acknowledgement on the copy and send it back as proof of the notification. A small fee is usually payable.

IF BUYING WITHOUT A MORTGAGE

The formalities that remained in connection with Matthew's purchase were dealt with by Hodgson, Green & Co. If you are buying without a mortgage, you will have to attend to these formalities yourself. Firstly, the transfer must be stamped, within 30 days (even if no stamp duty is payable). Stamping can be done in person at one of the Inland Revenue stamp offices (look under Inland Revenue in the telephone book). All you have to do is to take form Stamps L(A) 451 with you. The clerks or enquiry department at the stamp office will assist you, if necessary.

It is possible to send deeds for stamping through the post, using form *Stamps 61* (obtainable from head post offices) which has to be completed and sent to The Controller of Stamps, Inland Revenue (D), (Direct Post Section), West Block, Barrington Road, Worthing, West Sussex, with the transfer and payment for the correct amount of stamp duty.

Secondly, you must send the documents (land certificate, or charge certificate together with form 53(Co); transfer; official certificate of search, form 94A) to the Land Registry, together with your application on form A4 to be registered as the new proprietor and a cheque for the Land Registry fees. Remember to lodge your application with the Land Registry before your priority period expires, even if this means not waiting for form 53(Co); it can be forwarded later. It usually takes about twelve weeks for the registration to be completed.

JUST TO MAKE SURE

You can check that all is well by filling in Land Registry form A44 and sending it to the Land Registry with a fee of £1. The office copy which the Land Registry sends in response should show you as the new proprietor.

Emma's right of occupation

Under the Matrimonial Homes Act 1983 a spouse (husband or wife) has a right of occupation (that is, right to live there) in the matrimonial home wholly owned by the other spouse. These rights are in addition to any interest he or she may have in the property by virtue of contributions made to the purchase price or subsequent improvements to the property.

The right of occupation can be protected, in the case of registered property, by registration of a notice. This is done on form 99, and a fee of £3 is payable. The land certificate does not have to be produced to the registrar to register this type of notice, and the consent of the owner-spouse is therefore not necessary. (Where the home is subject to a mortgage, the Land Registry will already have the land certificate, anyway, the building society or other lender being issued with a charge certificate.)

The effect of registering a notice is that all dealings with the home take effect subject to the interest that is protected, unless the non-owner spouse agrees to the notice being cancelled. In other words, a husband cannot sell the property over the wife's head (and vice versa). The owner-spouse will not be informed of the registration – the aim, supposedly, being to protect a spouse against an angry husband or wife.

Protection of a spouse's right of occupation in the matrimonial home by registration is usually described as a 'hostile registration', presumably because it implies lack of trust by one spouse in the other. This type of registration is rare, probably because it is not until a marriage goes wrong that the parties begin to think about their individual rather than joint rights.

Emma, being a very far-sighted and cautious woman, decided that she would apply for the registration of a notice against 14 Twintree Avenue on form 99. Since she did not own the house jointly with Matthew, this was a sensible way of ensuring that he could not sell or mortgage the house free from her interest in it, should their marriage take a turn for the worse.

STOP PRESS

In the budget speech on 13 March 1984, the Chancellor announced that the stepped system of stamp duty would be abolished and replaced with a straight one per cent levy on a purchase price over £30,000.

Previously (and at the time when Matthew Seaton bought 14 Twintree Avenue in the winter of 1983), stamp duty was levied in bands: ½% for purchases from £25,000 to £30,000; one per cent for those between £30,001 and £35,000, then 1½% for purchases up to £40,000 and 2% for any above £40,001. The entire cost of the transaction was chargeable at the highest rate (so that small differences in purchase price could lead to large differences in stamp duty, and it was worth seeing whether any part of the property that was being sold could be attributed to fixtures and fittings, to keep the transaction in a lower stamp duty band).

fees the buyer has to pay

The Land Registry fee starts at £8 for a house costing up to £4,000 and goes up by £5 per £2,000 of the price (up to a buying price of £100,000).
The rate of stamp duty is nil up to a buying price of £30,000 and 1% for a buying price of £30,001 and over.

The Building Societies Association's recommended fees for the building society's solicitor are based on the amount of the mortgage, not the price of the house; the building society's valuation fees are not on a scale.

some examples:

house price	stamp duty	Land Registry fee	building society's solicitor's fee (on amount of repayment mortgage)
£	£	£	£
10,000	nil	23	84 00
15,000	nil	38	100
17,500	nil	43	104.80
25,000	nil	63	116
27,000	nil	68	117.60
29,750	nil	73	120
30,250	302.50	78	120.40
32,000	320	78	120.80
40,000	400	98	122
45,000	450	113	123.60

selling

What follows will tell you how to do the conveyancing involved when you sell your house. As in the case of buying, the instructions are limited to the sale of a house with vacant possession (and not let to tenants) which is not newly-built and which is already registered at the Land Registry with freehold or leasehold title. Selling is really the mirror image of buying. To avoid repetition, it is assumed in what follows that the reader has become familiar with the process of buying – or at least has followed it by reading the description of what Matthew Seaton did when buying his house.

a buyer

The first step in any sale is to find a buyer. The book *Which? way to buy, sell and move house* gives detailed information on the various methods of obtaining this objective. You have now reached the stage where you have decided to sell your registered freehold or leasehold house, either independently or simultaneously with your purchase of another house. You have agreed a price and got the name and address of your buyer and his solicitor. Your buyer might have paid a small earnest deposit to your estate agents, which they will hold as stakeholders, or if you are selling privately he may offer you such a deposit.

You should accept his money and give him a written receipt but do make sure that the receipt, and any other writing you give or send to him or his solicitors at this stage, contains the words *subject to contract*. This will prevent a binding contract coming into force until you are ready. Remember that a conveyancing transaction is in two parts: the first is up to exchange of contracts; the second, from exchange of contracts to completion.

deeds and documents
The next stage in the sale is the preparation of the draft contract and for this you need the deeds of the property, in the case of registered land, the land certificate or the charge certificate.

Where there is no existing mortgage on the property, the land certificate will either be in your possession or deposited with your bank for safekeeping, or with the solicitor who acted for you on your purchase. You will probably be required to sign a receipt when you get it back.

If there is an existing mortgage, the charge certificate will be held by the building society or other lender. They will not give you the charge certificate: it represents the security for the loan, and they will insist on keeping it until they are repaid in full. They will hand over the charge certificate to a seller's solicitor, but only on his giving a written undertaking to hold it on behalf of the lender and not to part with it to a third party until the lender has been repaid in full. Anyway, all you really need at this stage is the registered title number of your property (which your lender will let you know on request) so that you can obtain an office copy of the entries on the register from the Land Registry.

If you had a solicitor when you bought your house, it is as well to write to him for all the old papers. These may be of help to you later when you have to deal with your buyer's enquiries about the property. Provided that all the legal fees have been paid, you are entitled to be sent all your documents in your solicitor's file, except notes prepared by the solicitor for his own benefit and letters written to him by you. But, strictly speaking, solicitors need to keep papers for only 6 years.

GETTING OFFICE COPIES
Any copy document which has to be sent to the buyer's solicitor with the draft contract should be an office copy; it is the current practice amongst sellers' solicitors (and also a Law Society recommendation) to send a complete set of office copy entries to the other side at this stage. So, even if

you have the land certificate in your possession you should apply for and obtain an office copy of the entries on the register and the filed plan.

The form for applying for this is A44, called *Application for Office Copies*, available from Oyez shops. You should apply for a 'Complete set with Title plan' by putting the number you require in the appropriate box (box A). Only you, or people with your permission, may apply for an office copy of the register, so you must put a cross in the square at the top of the form declaring 'I am/We are the registered proprietor(s)'. The fee for obtaining a complete set with title plan is £3. This can be paid by cheque or by postal order or by means of special Land Registry stamps which may be bought from head post offices. The form should be sent to the district land registry which covers the district your property is in. The office copies will be sent to you by post after a few days.

It may be a good idea to ask for two copies of the entries on the register and filed plan, so that you will always have one copy on your file for reference throughout the sale transaction.

A seller who is really anxious to get things moving can also apply for a local search in advance on form LLC1 and form Con 29A (form Con 29D for London). Such a search is transferable, and can be used by the buyer. In areas where there is a considerable delay in getting a reply from the local authority, this can be a useful step.

the draft contract

Most solicitors in England and Wales use printed forms of contract, either the National Conditions of Sale or the General Conditions published by the Law Society. These forms used to be jealously guarded by the profession and not sold to non-solicitors. Now they are also made available to the general public. But if you should have difficulties in obtaining a standard form of contract, either the standard National or the Law Society's general conditions of sale (appearing on the inside two pages of these forms) can be included, by reference, into the seller's own form of contract, without infringing any copyright.

Here (on pages 110 and 111) is a specimen form of contract. It should be typed out on an ordinary piece of paper (with two carbon copies).

contract for the sale of a house with a registered title

The seller(s) agree(s) to sell and the buyer(s) agree(s) to buy the house described overleaf. The name(s) and address of the seller(s) and of the buyer(s) and the price agreed appear overleaf.

The sale is subject to the following conditions.

1. **Either** A deposit of ten per cent of the price is to be paid to AB (estate agents) of XYZ (address) on exchange of contracts and shall be held by them as stakeholders.

   or A deposit of ten per cent of the price is to be paid on exchange of contracts and shall be held in a joint account to be opened in the name of the seller and of the buyer or his solicitors at the branch of the bank stated overleaf. Cheques drawn on the account must be signed by both parties.
2. The seller(s) sell(s) as beneficial owner(s).
3. The property is sold subject to the rights, exceptions and reservations and covenants referred to in the property register and entries numbers ..... in the charges register, copies of which having been given to the buyer(s) or his solicitor, no objections shall be made or questions asked in respect thereof.
4. The seller's title shall be shown by supplying an office copy of the entries on the register and filed plan and an authority to inspect the register.
5. Vacant possession will be given on completion, the date for which is stated overleaf.
6. The property is used as a dwelling house in the occupation of one family and this is the permitted use thereof for the purposes of the Planning Acts.
7. **Either** The National Conditions of Sale (20th Edition) shall apply to this contract, except that condition 3 shall not have effect, and the agreed rate of interest shall be 11 per cent or 2 per cent above the base rate of .... Bank from time to time, whichever shall be the higher.

   or The Law Society's General Conditions of Sale (1980 Edition) shall apply to this contract, except that general condition 4 shall not apply, and the contract rate shall be 11 per cent, or 2 per cent above the base rate of .... Bank from time to time, whichever shall be the higher.

(back of form of contract)

Seller's full name(s) ....
address(es) ....
....
Buyer's full name(s) ....
address(es) ....
....
Description of the property: freehold/leashold house
   known as ....
Price...................................pounds (£   )

The property is registered at the Land Registry with title absolute/good
leasehold title under title number ....

Leasehold only: date of lease ....
made between .... and ....
original term of the lease .... years from ....
number of years now unexpired ....
ground rent £........ per year. Copy of the lease herewith.
Insurance company ....
address ....
policy number ....sum for which insured £.........
annual premium £........ date for renewal ....

Bank to hold deposit in joint names ....
address ....
Buyer's solicitors ....
address ....
completion date ....
signed ....date ....

The suggested form of contract provides for the incorporation by
reference of either the National or Law Society conditions of sale; which of
these you choose to incorporate is a matter of personal preference. The
form is also suitable for use by a sole or by joint owners. Where joint
owners are selling, both must be a party to the contract and the eventual
transfer.

If you are selling through an estate agent, the contractual ten per cent deposit can be paid to the agent as stakeholder. If not, you can suggest opening a special joint account at a bank. Your own bank or the buyer's solicitor's bank would both be appropriate. The account could be in the joint names of the seller and buyer or, more likely, the seller and the buyer's solicitor. The arrangement about drawing money from this joint account should be that both parties must sign cheques. The deposit is paid into this account by the buyer and stays there until the sale is completed. On completion, the buyer's solicitor hands over a cheque drawn on the joint account signed by the buyer or his solicitor. The seller then counter-signs the cheque and presents it in the normal way. The joint account is then closed.

Details of the restrictive covenant entries on the charges register can be found in your office copies. You do not refer to any mortgage you may have taken out on the security of the property, because it will have to be discharged on completion and you do not sell subject to it. Your office copies will also help you to fill in the blanks on the back of the suggested form.

Where the property is leasehold, you have to send a copy of the lease to the buyer's solicitor with the draft contract. If the property is not subject to a mortgage, you will have the lease with the land certificate. If it is subject to a mortgage, the building society or other lender will hold the lease, but will provide you with a copy of it (if you do not have one already) on payment of a small charge. The particulars of the lease that have to be given in the draft contract will appear in the lease itself. Details of insurance (required only in the case of a leasehold house) can be obtained from the last receipt for the annual premium.

DO NOT LET THE BUYER IN TOO SOON

It is usual to leave the completion date blank in the draft contract, to be filled in on exchange of contracts. Obviously, it would be foolish to let a buyer into possession before contracts are exchanged. Sometimes a buyer is anxious to take possession of the property as quickly as possible. But even if the buyer has signed a binding contract, he should not be allowed to take possession before completion: it might encourage him to delay it. Furthermore, a seller might have difficulties in regaining possession of a house from a buyer who was allowed in before completion, but who then refuses or is unable to complete his purchase.

Under both the National and Law Society's conditions of sale, if a buyer is let into possession before completion, he does so as a licensee not as a tenant. This excludes any protection conferred by the Rent Acts. He must pay all outgoings (rates, water rates and so on), and also interest on the balance of the purchase price, at the 'agreed' or 'contract' rate (National condition 8; Law Society's general condition 18).

Although not technically necessary until after exchange of contracts, it is a good idea to send a full set of office copy entries on the register and filed plan to the buyer's solicitor with the draft contract. Not only does it save time and trouble later, but if by any chance you have misunderstood some aspect of the matter or inaccurately transposed the information given in the register in filling in the draft contract, any such errors will be evident to the buyer's solicitor before contracts are exchanged; he cannot then later complain that he was misled by the way in which the contract was worded. If you bought your house before 1976 and you do not wish your buyer to know the price you paid for it, cut out the figure in the office copy of the proprietorship register before you send it off.

If you managed to obtain either the National or the Law Society's contract for sale, you should complete two copies of it as explained at pages 19 to 29. Then send one copy of it to the buyer's solicitor, together with the office copies of the entries on the register and filed plan. If not, type out two copies of the contract form suggested on pages 110 and 111, and send one of those with the office copies. In either case, you must retain one copy of the draft contract (which you will later exchange with the buyer). At this stage, neither copy should be signed or dated. In the covering letter you write to the buyer's solicitor, do not forget to incorporate the words 'subject to contract'.

enquiries before contract

After the buyer's solicitor has received your draft contract form, he will send you his preliminary enquiries probably on form Conveyancing 29 Long LM (Revised) – *Enquiries before Contract*. The extent of the seller's duty of disclosure of matters relevant to the property is discussed at page 43 and an explanation of the meaning and relevance of the enquiries on the printed form on 44 to 47. Try to be as helpful and informative as you can in answering the questions put to you, but remember that if you say something about the property which turns out to be untrue after exchange of contracts, it may amount to a misrepresentation entitling the buyer to terminate the contract and/or claim damages. If you have obtained your old purchase file from your solicitor who acted when you bought the house, you may find the preliminary enquiries then asked, and the replies then given. These will help you to reply to the present enquiries.

But if there are any questions you cannot understand, ask the buyer's solicitor to explain them to you.

Somewhere in the enquiries you will be asked if there is anyone living in the property who is not a party to the sale, and if so the nature of his or her interest, if any. If your wife/husband or anyone else (not being a co-owner) is living with you, they will either have to sign the contract to show that they submit to the sale, or sign an undertaking in similar form to the one shown on page 46.

After you have replied to the enquiries before contract, there is likely to be a lull in the transaction. The buyer now makes his local searches, has the house surveyed, arranges insurance and, if necessary, waits for his mortgage offer to come through.

During this period there is likely to be some correspondence between you (remember to include the words *subject to contract*) and the buyer's solicitor about the draft contract. He may urge that the contract be framed quite differently from that which you suggested, or he may accept your basis entirely. It is generally up to the seller to determine the terms on which he will sell. The buyer's solicitor may suggest the addition or alteration of one or two clauses to cover various points. But in the sale of a second-hand house with a registered title there should be little difficulty in agreeing the form of the contract.

If the buyer encounters difficulty in getting a mortgage or in selling his house, there may well be delay and frustration at this stage. If this goes on, you will have to decide whether to continue with this sale or find another buyer.

Before preparing your engrossment of the contract, be quite sure that it is in the form that both you and the buyer's solicitor have agreed. If no amendments or only very minor ones have been made, you can use as your engrossment the top copy of the draft contract which the buyer's solicitor has returned approved. Remember that the contract for the sale of a house really consists of two separate identical documents, one of which is signed by the seller and the other by the buyer.

exchange of contracts
It is the custom for the buyer's solicitor to send his client's signed contract to the seller first. This he will do once he has received back his local search certificate and replies to enquiries, and once the buyer has received a satisfactory surveyor's report and mortgage offer. (This is usually about six weeks after the buyer first offered to buy the property.)

When you receive the contract, check carefully that it is in the form you have agreed and that the buyer's signature (or signatures if there are more than one) appear at the end. Also check that the buyer has paid the 10 per cent deposit to the estate agent or into the joint account.

The contract signed by the buyer will be undated. Up to this point, either you or your buyer can still call the deal off, without giving any reason.

Before sending your signed contract to the buyer's solicitor, date both contracts with the date of exchange. If necessary, also fill in the completion date on both. This date is usually four weeks after exchange and you will probably already have agreed a completion date with your buyer.

The contract becomes binding between you and the buyer the moment when you, having received the buyer's signed contract, post to the buyer's solicitor an identical contract signed by yourself and your husband/wife (or other person) if co-owners. Each party or his solicitor then holds a separate identical contract signed by the other and an exchange of contracts has been effected.

WHAT YOU MUST SEND
You will already have sent a complete office copy of the entries on the register and filed plan to the buyer's solicitor with the draft contract, so all you need send him now, with your signed contract, is an authority to inspect the register, to fulfil your duty to prove your title. But if by any chance you did not send a complete set of office copy entries on the register with the draft contract, now is the time to do so.

An authority to inspect the register can be done on form 201, obtainable from Oyez shops. It is easy to fill in and must be signed by you (and any co-owner) as registered proprietor. It should be worded so as to allow the buyer's solicitor to inspect the register, because he will need it when he makes his official search of the register (on form 94A or B) a week before completion.

A letter addressed to the Land Registry can be used instead of form 201.

135 Thackeray Villas
Picklebridge, Lancs

3rd March 1983

To: The Chief Land Registrar
The Lytham District Land Registry
Lytham St Annes
Lancs.

Dear Sir,

Title No. LA 24689753
135 Thackeray Villas, Picklebridge

Please permit Messrs Forbes, Wainwright & Spencer, solicitors of Bank Chambers, High Street, Blakeford to inspect the register relating to the above title.

Yours faithfully,

Herbert Reginald Oaks
(registered proprietor)

chain transactions

It happens fairly often that a person who is selling his home must make sure that he has another to move to. Conversely, a buyer needs to be sure that he has sold his house before he buys another. In this way, a number of transactions can be linked together to form a chain. Some fine timing is often necessary to resolve this situation. (The solution to this problem of simultaneous exchange of contracts by telephone is not recommended to a person doing his own conveyancing.)

Remember that if you are both buying a new house and selling your present one, you should not send off the signed contract for your purchase until you have received your buyer's signed contract for the house you are selling. Once you have received your signed contract of sale, a bridging loan might provide you with the answer to finding the deposit which you need for your purchase.

Even after exchange of contracts there might be difficulty in synchronising completion dates, in the case of interdependent sales and purchases. Again, your bank may be willing to give you a temporary bridging loan to enable you to complete the purchase of your new home before you complete the sale of your present one. But the bank will only be willing to do this after you have a binding contract of sale on your present home. The bank will also probably require a solicitor's undertaking to remit part of the sale money to them once the sale has been completed; the amount necessary to repay the loan and interest. It should not be too difficult for you to pesuade your buyer's solicitor to give your bank such an undertaking, although he will probably charge you a small fee for doing so. If you do manage to get a loan from the bank, make sure that when the loan is granted it is expressed in such terms as to be eligible for tax relief (an ordinary bank overdraft or personal loan is not).

preparing to pay off the mortgage

As soon as you have exchanged contracts with a buyer, and are therefore in a position to assume the sale will go through, you should contact your building society or other lender to let them know that you will shortly be wanting to pay off your outstanding mortgage. If you know your completion date, you can specify that as being the date you will be paying off the mortgage.

Many mortgages contain a clause saying that you must give three months' notice (or some other length of time) of your intention to pay off the loan. This means that you will have to pay interest on the outstanding loan (but not capital repayments) up to a day three months from the date on which you give official notice to the building society. This clause used to be very strictly enforced by building societies, but you may well find this is no longer so. However, the sooner you give notice, the less you will have to pay by way of interest if the early redemption charge is imposed. If anything should happen to delay the sale of your house, you can withdraw your notice to the building society.

Some building societies waive the redemption charges for people who apply for another mortgage for the new house they are buying.

When you write to your lender, ask exactly how much money will be required to pay off the mortgage on the day fixed for completion. If yours is a repayment (as against an endowment) mortgage, you can, in fact, work out yourself how much you still owe by following the calculations on page 133 of the Consumer Publication *Raising the money to buy your home*. This is particularly useful, also, to work out what would happen if there should be a delay to the completion date, in which case there would need to be an adjustment in the amount the building society requires to pay off the mortgage. Many building societies, when notifying a mortgagor of the amount required to pay off the loan on a given date, also state the amount of interest that will accrue each day after that, so that the borrower does not have to go back to the building society for a recalculation if completion is slightly delayed.

requisitions on title

Shortly after exchange of contracts, the buyer's solicitor will send you his requisitions on title probably on form Con 28B. A consideration of the meaning and relevance of the requisitions and the time limits for making and replying to them appears at pages 65–67.

Firstly, you will be asked to confirm that there has been no variation to the answers you gave to the preliminary enquiries. If there has not, your reply should be 'The seller is not aware of any variation'. If there has been a change, the details should be given.

Secondly, you will be asked to produce, at completion, receipts for any outgoings you intend to apportion in your completion statement.

You need not answer 3(B), as a recent office copy of the entries on the register will have been sent by you to the buyer.

Question 4 deals with mortgages and states that all subsisting mortgages must be discharged on or before completion. You obviously confirm this. Then it asks whether 'the vacating receipt, discharge of registered charge, or consent to dealing' will be handed over on completion. The 'discharge of registered charge' applies to the sale of a registered house within the scope of this book. If your lender is a company or a building society the discharge will be on form 53(Co); if a private individual form 53. Often a building society does not hand over form 53(Co) at completion, but an undertaking to do so. Question 4(B)(ii) therefore asks for the proposed terms of such an undertaking. A solicitor's undertaking is something special. Provided that it is not qualified in any way, it puts the solicitor under a personal obligation to carry it out, even if his client defaults. If a buyer and/or his building society or other lender is not to be handed form 53(Co) on completion, he or his solicitor will only be content with your building society's (or other lender's) solicitor's personal and unqualified undertaking to forward form 53(Co) to him within a specified period, usually 14 days.

Requisition 5 states that vacant possession must be given on completion. This has already been agreed in the contract and should be agreed. It then asks if every person in occupation of the property has agreed to vacate it before or on completion. The answer to this question is important to a buyer: he must ensure that he will not be saddled with any overriding interests once he becomes the registered proprietor of the house. The question then asks about keys; arrangements about these can be made later.

Question 7 asks for details regarding actual completion. You will probably not be able to supply these until a later date.

Then may follow extra questions relevant to your particular sale. For example, if your wife or husband had registered a notice (which would appear on the office copy entries) protecting her/his right of occupation in the property under the Matrimonial Homes Act 1983, you might be asked here to confirm that you will hand over a form signed by your wife or husband stating she or he consents to cancellation of the notice.

The requisitions on title may, instead of being on a printed form, be the buyer's solicitor's own home-made variety. They should present no problem, but if you do not understand any of the questions, ask the buyer's solicitor to explain them.

Finally sign and date the requisitions at the end of the form and send it back to the buyer's solicitor, keeping the copy for your file.

the transfer

The buyer's solicitor usually sends, with his requisitions, the draft transfer for your approval, together with a copy for your use. The transfer will almost invariable be on form 19 *Transfer of whole*, and will follow exactly the lines of the transfer to Matthew Seaton on page 69. So simple is this form that there is usually little room for amendments, and you will be invited to treat the top copy of the transfer as the engrossment, to be executed by you and handed over at completion.

Where the transfer is to the buyers as joint proprietors, form 19(JP) will be used. The transfer will contain a clause regulating the joint owners' rights between themselves but this need not concern you. The only difference it will make is that you will have to return the top copy to the buyers' solicitor (if approved by you and thus treated as the engrossment) for execution by his clients. He will then return it for you to execute and hand over at completion.

You should check the details written onto the transfer form and provided these are correct you can approve it. If form 19 (as opposed to 19(JP)) has been used, all you need do is write to the buyer's solicitor saying that you approve the draft transfer. You keep the top copy for use as the engrossment, and also the carbon copy of the transfer for your file.

buyer's building society (or other lender)

If a buyer is obtaining part of the purchase price on mortgage, he will have to deal with his building society's (or other lender's) requisitions on title (see page 76). Where the same solicitor is acting for the buyer and the lender, he will incorporate the lender's requisitions into the requisitions on title he sends to the seller on Con 28B, so killing two birds with one stone.

Where different solicitors act for the lender and the buyer, you may find that you get another set of requisitions to answer, put by the lender's solicitor. The buyer's solicitor may say 'My clients mortgagees have raised the following requisitions in addition to those which you have already answered and I shall be glad if you will let me have replies'.

It is highly likely that these requisitions will, technically, be out of time. Under the National Conditions requisitions must be made within 11 working days of the receipt (by the buyer) of the office copy entries or the date of the contract, whichever is the later. The Law Society's contract, or one incorporating its conditions, stipulates a 6 working days period. Technically, you are entitled to refuse to answer requisitions that are made out of time, but it would be highly unusual to refuse to answer these additional questions on this ground. The lender's requisitions will probably be similar to those you have already answered and should not cause any difficulty.

preparing for completion

About ten days before completion, you will have to prepare and send to your buyer's solicitor a completion statement, showing the exact amount of money you require at completion. (For an example of the form of a completion statement, see page 86.) This amount basically consists of the price agreed, less any deposit paid by the buyer, plus or minus an apportionment of general and water rates and water services charges depending on whether at the date of completion it is in arrears or has been paid in advance. In the case of leasehold property, ground rent, insurance and service charges are apportioned.

APPORTIONMENTS

The rule is that the seller is responsible for outgoings up to and including the day before completion, while the buyer is responsible for outgoings from and including the actual completion day. In calculating the apportionment of these outgoings, you may have to find out the date to which each has already been paid. This will be shown on the demand for the most recent payment you made. Receipts are not given for general and water rates and water services charges unless specially requested. If you know you will be selling, you should ask for receipts because you may need to produce them at completion. Alternatively you can get a letter from the local and water authorities confirming the date to which rates and charges are paid, and the amounts.

General rates and water rates and water services charges and insurance (if your house is leasehold) are generally paid in advance, so that when it comes to completion they should already be paid up to a date later than the agreed completion date. If this is the case, you have to work out how much of the payment made is for the period between completion day and the last day covered by the payment; the buyer is responsible for payment of this amount and it should therefore be added to the amount he has to pay on completion.

Ground rent for a leasehold house is usually paid in arrears. As a result, the apportionment of ground rent is usually in favour of the buyer; that is, something has to be subtracted from the money needed to complete, to cover the proportion of ground rent for the period for which no ground rent has yet been paid.

It is not, in fact, necessary for the general water rate and water services charges to be apportioned. You can write to the various rating and water authorities informing them of your sale and the completion date, and the full name of the buyer, and asking them to give you an apportioned figure up to completion. If you have paid in advance you will get a refund. If not the buyer's solicitor will probably require you to give them an undertaking (on completion), to pay these up to completion. This can be in the form of a simple letter addressed to the buyer's solicitors promising to pay the relevant outgoings and stating the amount.

If the house has been empty for any length of time during which no rates have had to be paid, the seller should produce a receipt at completion, showing that the rates have been paid up to the date when the house was last occupied.

If the buyer has, exceptionally, been allowed into possession before completion (to carry out some repairs or decorating perhaps), the completion statement, besides apportioning the outgoings as from the date on which the buyer was allowed in, rather than at the date of completion, will include an item for the interest on the balance of the purchase price. It is worked out on a daily basis: so-many three hundred and sixty-fifths of one year's interest at the appropriate rate per cent on the price less deposit.

HOW TO GET THE MONEY

Either on the completion statement or within the next few days, you should tell the buyer's solicitor exactly how you require the completion monies to be paid. Where you are paying off an existing mortgage, you should have found out how much money will be needed to pay off the mortgage on the day fixed for completion. You should also have asked whether the banker's draft for the amount should be made payable to the building society (or other lender) itself or to its solicitors. With this information, you can work out how the completion monies must be split: so much to the building society or other lender (or its solicitors) – the remainder to yourself.

It might, however, be more complicated than that. For instance, you may be completing the purchase of another house on the same day as you are completing the sale, using whatever is left after paying off your old mortgage to help pay for the house you are buying. Your seller's solicitors may have asked you to pay the money you are providing at the completion of your purchase in two separate amounts. Furthermore, you may be having a fresh mortgage on the house you are buying and the amount to be advanced must be taken into account, too. The answer is keep calm and work it all out step by step.

The buyer's money is probably coming from at least two sources, too. If he is having a mortgage, and you are paying one off, you may expect that the completion monies will in fact be split at least 3 ways and 3 banker's drafts will be produced at completion. (This is what happened at the completion of Matthew Seaton's purchase of 14 Twintree Avenue.)

WHERE TO COMPLETE

You must also agree a venue for completion. If you have no existing mortgage to pay off, the buyer's solicitor's office will be the most likely place. If a mortgage is to be paid off, completion usually takes place at the seller's building society's (or other lender's) solicitor's office.

You should ask for completion to take place before 2.30pm on the completion day, so that banking arrangements can be made on the same day.

Where the parties live some distance apart, completion is often carried out through the post. However, your buyer's solicitor may not agree to complete through the post with a seller acting on his own behalf, so if you have an existing mortgage, your mortgagee's solicitor could be asked to act as your agent for a postal completion.

BEFORE COMPLETION

Finally, in readiness for completion, you should execute the transfer. This involves signing the transfer in the space indicated (alongside the 'seal', which is a little round red sticker) in the presence of a witness, who should countersign the transfer and add his or her name, address and occupation. Any co-seller should also execute the transfer in the same way. The transfer should be left undated until completion.

For the seller, there are no complicated preparations for completion. You will usually only have to take along the transfer. If you have no mortgage you will have to provide the land certificate (and the lease, in the case of a leasehold house). You may also have to produce evidence of payment of outgoings for the buyer's solicitor to inspect, and of course hand over the keys.

It may well happen that the buyer (or someone on his behalf) asks if he can inspect the property before, or on, the morning of the completion day. You should make arrangements for him to do this, as it is an important part of his pre-completion preparations.

You should also make some arrangement about the fees of the solicitors for the building society (or other lender) whose existing mortgage is paid off, if this is the case. These fees will have to be met by you, the borrower. There is no scale fee. Not much legal work is involved in the redemption of a mortgage, and the fee will probably be in the region of £25. You should agree the amount beforehand and will probably be asked to pay it at completion.

completion

The procedure followed at completion will be similar to that followed at the completion of Matthew Seaton's purchase of 14 Twintree Avenue (see pages 101–103).

The solicitors of your mortgagee will probably begin the proceedings by handing the charge certificate to you. Make sure that it is the right one and hand it to the buyer's solicitor. The same procedure usually applies to form 53 or 53(Co) or an undertaking to provide it. If you have no existing mortgage to pay off, hand over the land certificate instead.

Next comes the transfer. This will be undated and you should confirm that the buyer's solicitor wishes that the transfer should bear the date on which completion is taking place. Very occasionally there may be a reason why the transfer should be dated some other day.

By and large, however, you are wise to insist that the transfer bears the date of completion. When you have dated the transfer, hand it to the buyer's solicitor. He will then pass it to his client's mortgagee's solicitor with the mortgage deed and any other items required. At this stage, you might also be required to show the buyer's solicitor receipts or other evidence that any relevant outgoings have been paid and/or hand over an undertaking to pay any outstanding bills for them.

GETTING THE MONEY

Now the money is paid over. The buyer's solicitor will produce banker's drafts totalling the amount required to complete, as set out on your completion statement. Check that they are made out as you requested. If you are discharging a mortgage hand over to your lender's solicitor the draft that is made payable to your lender (or his solicitor).

Finally, the deposit has to be made over to you. If it was paid to an estate agent as stakeholder you will require a deposit release from the buyer's solicitor. Immediately after completion, you must write to the estate agent sending him the deposit release and asking him to send you a cheque for the deposit. If he acted as agent on the sale of your house, you will find that he deducts his commission for the sale from the amount of the deposit.

If the deposit has been held in a joint account at a bank, in the name of say the buyer's solicitor and yourself, the buyer's solicitor should hand you a cheque signed by him drawn on the joint account. You then countersign the cheque and present it in the normal way, and the account is closed.

The buyer is entitled to take possession of the house immediately the sale is completed. You should therefore now hand the keys to the buyer's solicitor. If it is more convenient, leave them with the estate agent and hand to the buyer's solicitor a letter addressed to the estate agents authorising them to hand the keys to the buyer.

If by any chance completion is delayed, the procedure described on page 103 is applicable to both sales and purchases.

AFTERWARDS

After completion, do not forget to cancel the insurance (except in the case of a leasehold house, where the insurance is generally taken over by the buyer). Strictly speaking you could have cancelled the insurance as soon as contracts were exchanged, as the house was the buyer's responsibility from then on. But it is best to maintain the insurance until the money is in your hands. And remember, too, to have the electricity and gas meters read on the day you move out and to notify the post office regarding the telephone and to cancel the instructions to your bank if you have been paying your lender by banker's order. These however are practical matters: the legal side of selling the house is over.

glossary

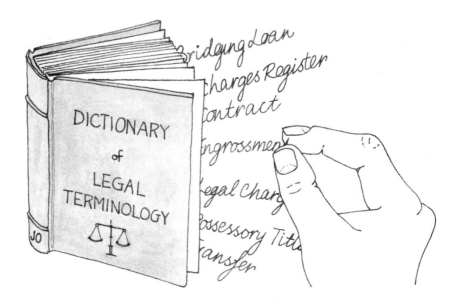

AUTHORITY TO INSPECT THE REGISTER: the document, addressed to the Land Registry, by which the registered proprietor, that is the owner, allows someone else, usually the buyer's solicitor, to be given information about the register of a property, usually to enable him to make an official search.

BANKER'S DRAFT: a cheque signed by a bank manager, or one of his staff. As it is signed on behalf of the bank, instead of by the customer, it is almost inconceivable that it would not be met and is treated in practice as being equivalent to cash.

BRIDGING LOAN: a loan, usually from a bank, to tide a person over between the time when he has to pay the purchase price of one house and the time when the proceeds of sale of another and/or mortgage funds become available to him.

CHARGE: any right or interest, subject to which freehold or leasehold property may be held, especially a mortgage; also used to denote a debit, or a claim for payment.

CHARGE CERTIFICATE: the certificate issued by the Land Registry to the mortgagee of a property which has a registered title, showing what is entered on the register of the property at the Land Registry. (When there is no mortgage, a land certificate is issued instead to the registered proprietor.)

CHARGES REGISTER: one of the three parts (the others are the property register and the proprietorship register) which go to make up the register at the Land Registry of a property with a registered title. The charges register contains details of restrictive covenants, mortgages and other interests, subject to which the registered proprietor owns the property.

CHATTELS: moveable possessions, such as furniture, clothes, jewellery, cars.

COMPLETION: the culmination of the procedure in the transfer of a house, when the necessary documents are handed over in exchange for the purchase money.

COMPLETION STATEMENT: an account prepared by the seller (or his solicitor), setting out exactly how much money he claims should be paid by the buyer at completion, taking into account the price, the deposit and the apportionments.

COMPULSORY REGISTRATION OF TITLE: the requirement in certain parts of England and Wales that any property, when next bought, should be registered at the Land Registry.

CONDITIONS OF SALE: the detailed standard terms which govern the rights and duties of the buyer and the seller of a house, as laid down in the contract which they sign. These may be the National or the Law Society's conditions of sale.

CONTRACT: any legally binding agreement; on the sale of a house this is the document, in two identical parts, one signed by the buyer and the other by the seller, which, when the parts are exchanged, commits both the buyer and the seller to complete the transaction by transferring ownership in exchange for paying the purchase money.

CONVEYANCING: that part of a solicitor's work which is concerned with the transfer of real property and with rights and interests in connection with it.

COVENANT: a promise in a deed.

DEED: a legal document which, instead of being merely signed, is 'signed, sealed and delivered'. This can have a special significance; for example, a promise getting nothing in return is only enforceable in law if it is made in the form of a deed. The legal title to freehold and leasehold property can only be transferred by a deed.

DELIVERY: the handing over of a deed, after having been signed and sealed, with the intention that it should now be operative.

DEPOSIT: part of the purchase price, usually ten per cent, which the buyer pays on or before exchange of contracts. It is usually held by the seller's solicitors as stakeholders (sometimes a small part of it by the estate agent). It can be forfeited to the seller if the buyer withdraws (through no fault on the part of the seller) after signing a binding contract.

DEPOSIT RELEASE: a letter signed by the buyer or his solicitor which permits the estate agents, if they hold a deposit, to hand it over to the seller, once the sale is completed.

DISCHARGE OF REGISTERED CHARGE: a document by which a building society, or other mortgagee, acknowledges that all the money secured by a mortgage on a registered property has been paid. It is usually made on the printed form known as form 53(Co).

ENGROSSMENT: the actual deed or document which is executed or signed, as opposed to a mere draft of it.

ENQUIRIES BEFORE CONTRACT: a collection of detailed questions about many aspects of a property which the seller, or his solicitor, is generally asked to answer before the buyer is prepared to sign a contract. Also called preliminary enquiries.

ENQUIRIES OF LOCAL AUTHORITY: a number of questions asked of a local authority on a printed form about a particular property. The form is usually sent with, and loosely speaking forms part of, the buyer's local search which is made before contracts are exchanged.

EXCHANGE OF CONTRACTS: the stage in the transfer of a house at which the buyer signs an engrossment of the contract and sends it to the seller, and the seller does the same in return, so that both become legally bound to go through with the transaction. Many solicitors 'exchange' over the telephone, but usually not with a do-it-yourself conveyancer.

EXECUTE: to sign and seal a document.

FEE SIMPLE: freehold.

FILED PLAN: the Land Registry plan by reference to which a particular registered property is identified in the property register.

FIXTURES: articles, such as radiators, baths and tv aerials, which, because they are attached (by screws, concrete or pipes, for instance) to the house itself, as opposed to standing supported by their own weight, are presumed to have become legally part of the house itself, so that they are included in a sale, unless specifically excluded by the contract.

FORM 53(Co): the form on which a mortgagee acknowledges that a mortgage of a property with a registered title has been paid off; the discharge of a registered charge. Where the lender is an individual (not a building society or company) form 53 is used.

FREEHOLD: the absolute ownership of property, as opposed to leasehold.

GOOD LEASEHOLD TITLE: the description given by the Land Registry to the title or ownership of a leasehold property having a registered title, where the Registry is entirely satisfied about the owner's entitlement to the lease itself, but has not enquired into the ownership of the freehold or other superior title of that property. In practice, good leasehold title is treated as being as good as title absolute.

GROUND RENT: the rent paid to the landlord by a leaseholder who owns a leasehold property. Ground rent for a house is often for not more than £20 a year, and the lease, when first granted, was for a long period, say 99 or even 999 years.

JOINT TENANTS: two (or more) people who hold property jointly in such a way that, when one dies, the whole property automatically passes to the survivor. This is in contrast with what happens in the case of tenants in common.

LAND CHARGES REGISTRY: a government department in Plymouth which keeps a register, open to public search, of certain charges on land in England and Wales the title to which is unregistered. It is quite distinct from the Land Registry, which deals only with properties where the title is registered. Charges are registered against the name of the owner, not the land concerned.

LAND CERTIFICATE: the certificate issued to the registered proprietor of a property which has a registered title, showing what is entered on the register of that property at the Land Registry. When the property is mortgaged, no land certificate is issued (it is retained at the Land Registry) and instead a charge certificate is issued to the mortgagee.

LAND REGISTRY: a government department whose head office is in London. District registries in various other places in England and Wales are responsible for opening, maintaining and amending the registers of all properties in England and Wales which have registered titles. Not to be confused with the Land Charges Registry, which deals with properties which have unregistered titles.

LAW SOCIETY: the professional body governing solicitors. As well as looking after their interests, the Law Society maintains professional discipline over solicitors.

LAW SOCIETY'S CONDITIONS OF SALE: one of the available sets of standard terms which may be incorporated into a contract for the sale of a house and so govern the rights of the buyer and the seller; another such set is the National Conditions of Sale.

LEASEHOLD: ownership of property for a fixed number of years granted by a lease which sets out the obligations of the leaseholder, for example regarding payment of rent to the landlord, repairs and insurance; as opposed to freehold property, where ownership is absolute.

LEASEHOLDER: the person who, for the time being, owns a leasehold property. He can apply to the landlord to buy the freehold, and become the freeholder, if his lease is for more than 21 years.

LEGAL CHARGE: a mortgage, especially one framed so as to include the words 'legal charge'.

LESSEE: the person to whom a lease was originally granted, and, more commonly, the present leaseholder.

LESSOR: the person who originally granted a lease; also, the present landlord.

LICENCE: permission to do something which, without it, would be illegal.

LICENCE TO ASSIGN: permission from a landlord allowing the leaseholder to transfer his lease to a specified person, as required by a clause in the lease.

LOCAL AUTHORITY: the local council responsible for roads, planning, social services and many other local matters on which rates are spent. All areas have two local authorities: a district council and a county council (or metropolitan district council and a metropolitan county council). In London there is the GLC and the borough councils.

LOCAL SEARCH: an application made on a special form to the local authority (the district council, or in London the borough council) for a certificate providing certain information about a property in the area. Also denotes the search certificate itself. A local search should reveal whether the property is likely to be affected by compulsory purchase, whether there are any outstanding sanitary notices, and similar matters. Loosely speaking, a local search also includes the answers given by the local authority to a number of standard additional enquiries, made on another special form; these answers are usually obtained at the time when the local search is made, but technically they are not part of it.

L.A. FORM: the form on which a buyer provides particulars of his purchase to the Inland Revenue. This is done immediately following completion. This form is also known as a PD ('particulars delivered') form and officially as Stamps L(A) 451. It can be obtained from head post offices and Inland Revenue stamp offices.

MORTGAGE (sometimes called a legal charge): a deed whereby freehold or leasehold property is pledged as security for a loan. It gives to the lender (such as a building society) certain rights in the property, including the power to sell if the mortgage payments are not made. These rights are cancelled when the money advanced is repaid with interest, in accordance with the agreed terms.

MORTGAGEE: one who lends money on mortgage, such as a building society, bank, local authority, insurance company or private lender.

MORTGAGOR: one who borrows money on mortgage, usually to enable him to buy a house.

NATIONAL CONDITIONS OF SALE: one of the available sets of standard terms which may be incorporated into a contract for the sale of a house, so as to govern the rights of the buyer and the seller of a property; another set is the Law Society's conditions of sale.

OFFICE COPY: an authenticated copy of an official document issued by the department or organisation which holds the original.

OFFICIAL SEARCH: an application to an official authority (such as a local authority, the Land Registry or the Land Charges Registry), to find out some relevant facts about a particular property.

OVERRIDING INTEREST: rights which are enforceable against a property, even though they are not referred to on the register of the property at the Land Registry; for instance, the right of a weekly tenant to remain in possession after the house has been sold, even though no mention of his tenancy is found on the register.

POSSESSORY TITLE: the description given by the Land Registry to the title or ownership of a property where, due to some defect in the title, the registry is not entirely satisfied as to the owner's ownership of the property, but only satisfied that he is lawfully in possession of the property; as opposed to title absolute and good leasehold title.

PRELIMINARY ENQUIRIES: enquiries before contract.

PROPERTY REGISTER: one of the three parts (the other two being the proprietorship register and the charges register) of the register of a property with a registered title. The property register sets out an exact description of the property concerned.

PROPRIETORSHIP REGISTER: one of the three parts (the other two being the property register and the charges register) of the register of a property with a registered title. The proprietorship register sets out the name and address of the registered proprietor, that is, the present owner, and the price which he paid for the property.

REAL PROPERTY: land, in particular freehold land, and any buildings on it, especially when used in the legal sense.

REGISTER: in the case of a property with a registered title, the record for that property kept at the Land Registry, divided into the property, the proprietorship and the charges registers.

REGISTERED PROPRIETOR: the person who is the owner of a property which has a registered title and is shown as such in the proprietorship register at the Land Registry.

REGISTERED TITLE: title or ownership of freehold or leasehold property which has been registered at the Land Registry, with the result that ownership is guaranteed by the state. In some parts of the country, registration of title is compulsory.

RENTCHARGE: a sum periodically payable by the owner of property under a covenant; a chief rent.

REQUISITIONS FOR AN OFFICIAL SEARCH: an application, on the appropriate form, for an official search.

REQUISITIONS ON TITLE: questions asked in writing by or on behalf of a buyer or mortgagee about matters concerning the seller's ownership of the property, and about other matters arising after exchange of contracts, as opposed to enquiries before contract.

RESTRICTIVE COVENANTS: obligations imposed by covenants on the owner of a freehold property, preventing him from doing certain things on his property, such as opening a business or putting buildings on certain parts of it.

ROAD CHARGES: the charges imposed on the owners of properties along a road, usually according to the frontage of each property, for the cost of making up or repairing the road.

ROOT OF TITLE: one of the title deeds, generally at least 15 years old, with which a seller starts his abstract of title, with the result that he undertakes to prove ownership from that time down to the present; applies only to properties with unregistered titles.

SCALE FEE: a fee calculated by reference to the price being paid, or money being borrowed, rather than to the amount of work involved. There is no scale fee for solicitors' conveyancing work.

SEAL: a small paper disc stuck alongside the signature on a deed.

SEARCH: an enquiry for, or an inspection of, information recorded by some official authority, such as a local authority, the Land Registry or the Land Charges Registry.

SEARCH CERTIFICATE: the certificate of the result of a search.

SOLICITOR'S UNDERTAKING: a letter signed by a solicitor in which he personally guarantees something, such as that his client's mortgage will be paid off. It is his professional duty to honour such an undertaking, even though he may suffer financially as a result if his client defaults.

STAKEHOLDER: one who holds a deposit as an intermediary between buyer and seller, so that the deposit may only be passed on to the seller with the permission of the buyer, or returned to the buyer with the permission of the seller.

STAMP DUTY: a duty payable to the government on some deeds and documents, including deeds of transfer, conveyance or assignment of property at a price above (at present) £30,000. Deeds and documents cannot be used as evidence or registered at the Land Registry unless they are properly stamped.

SUBJECT TO CONTRACT: provisionally agreed, but not so as to constitute a binding legal contract. If the buyer and the seller have agreed terms 'subject to contract', either may still back out without giving any reason.

TENANT FOR LIFE: a beneficiary who is entitled to receive the rent or other income from, or live in, property during his lifetime only, after which it will pass to others, in accordance with an existing will or trust.

TENANTS IN COMMON: two (or more) people who together hold property in such a way that, when one dies, his share does not pass automatically to the survivor but forms part of his own property and passes under his will or intestacy. This is in contrast with what happens in the case of joint tenants.

TITLE ABSOLUTE: the description given by the Land Registry to the title or ownership of a freehold (and sometimes leasehold) property where the registry is entirely satisfied about the owner's ownership of the property. Being registered with title absolute means that ownership is guaranteed by the state.

TITLE DEEDS: deeds and other documents which prove ownership of freehold or leasehold property. They normally consist of each deed transferring ownership over the previous fifteen years or more, together with mortgage deeds. Where the title is registered at the Land Registry, the title deeds are replaced by a land certificate (or, if there is a mortgage, by a charge certificate) issued by the Land Registry.

TRANSFER: a deed which transfers the ownership of a freehold or leasehold property, the title to which is registered at the Land Registry (as opposed to the deed used where the title is unregistered, which is a conveyance in the case of a freehold, and an assignment in the case of a leasehold).

TRUSTEE: a person in whom the legal ownership of property is vested, but who holds it for the benefit of someone else (called a beneficiary), such as a child.

TRUSTEES FOR SALE: people who hold property as trustees on condition that they should sell the property, but usually with a power to postpone doing so indefinitely if they want to.

VENDOR: the seller.

Consumer Publications

The list of CA's Consumer Publications includes:

Approaching retirement

Avoiding back trouble

Avoiding heart trouble

Central heating

Cutting your cost of living

Dealing with household emergencies

Earning money at home

Getting a new job

Living through middle age

Living with stress

Making the most of your freezer

On getting divorced (England and Wales)

Pregnancy month by month

Raising the money to buy your home

Securing your home

Starting your own business

The newborn baby

What to do when someone dies

Where to live after retirement

Which? 25 years on

Which? way to buy, sell and move house

Which? way to slim

Wills and probate (England and Wales)

CONSUMER PUBLICATIONS are available from
Consumers' Association, Castlemead, Gascoyne Way, Hertford SG14 1LH
and from booksellers.